Athapaskan Adaptations

WORLDS
OF
MAN

Studies in
Cultural Ecology

EDITED BY

Walter Goldschmidt

University of California
Los Angeles

Athapaskan Adaptations
Hunters and Fishermen of the Subarctic Forests

JAMES W. VANSTONE
FIELD MUSEUM OF NATURAL HISTORY / CHICAGO

AHM Publishing Corporation
Arlington Heights, Illinois 60004

Frontispiece: Koyukon caribou drive, 1860s
(from F. Whymper, *Voyages et Aventures dans
la Colombie Anglaise, L'Ile Vancouver, le
Territoire d'Alaska et la California*, Paris, Librairie
Hachette, 1880, p. 119).

Cover: An Indian leader from the Tanana River,
1926 (courtesy of National Anthropological
Archives, Smithsonian Institution).

ISBN: 0-88295-611-6
(Formerly 202-01114-3)

Library of Congress Card Number: 73-89518

PRINTED IN THE UNITED STATES OF AMERICA
747
Second Printing

FOR POLLY

The Author

James W. VanStone is Curator of North American Archaeology and Ethnology at the Field Museum of Natural History in Chicago. He is also Lecturer in the Department of Anthropology, Northwestern University. Professor VanStone received his M.A. and Ph.D. at the University of Pennsylvania and has been affiliated with the University of Toronto and the University of Alaska. He is the author of nine books and monographs, fifty articles, and many book reviews in anthropological journals.

Foreword

The great expanse of Arctic and Sub-Arctic lands that stretch across the northern edge of the American continent is as difficult and demanding to man as any in the world. The Athapaskan-speaking Indians who made it their home never captured the imagination of our popular writers, however, as did the Eskimo who lived on their northern borders and the Plains Indians who lived to the south. Except to anthropologists, the Athapaskans have remained in relative obscurity, known intimately only to the missionaries, the traders and trappers, and the prospectors who invaded their forbidding territory.

James VanStone has caught the elements of the basic adaptive strategy by which these Indians mastered their intransigent environment and made it their home over many centuries, and in doing so, he has perhaps also found the reasons why they have not had as much impact on Western thought as other native Americans. The Plains Indians, with the blood and thunder of their raidings, the individual drama of their vision quests, appealed to that part of our culture that was forged on the frontier where both action and isolation were primary qualities. The Eskimos, with their elaborate technology for extracting a livelihood from the Arctic ice appeal to Yankee ingenuity.

Athapaskan culture was of a different order—less dramatic, but no less adaptive. It involved, as VanStone says, a cultural flexibility, a quiet competence, a sustained ability to blend in with local environment. For these northern lands are not richly endowed with sustenance for human life, nor are they uniform. Men

, forbidden

had to find the particular resources on which they could build a life—here fishing, there trapping, elsewhere a single hunter following the lone moose or a coordinated group following herds of caribou, or more likely some combination of these varying with the seasons. These adaptations have not only required a proficiency in the tools and techniques for exploiting this difficult and diverse habitat, but also the creation of appropriate institutions for collaboration in these endeavors. Athapaskan social organization was adjusted to the different demands of these tasks, not only from one band to the next but seasonally within the same band. One surprising implication of this, in view of dominant anthropological thought, is that bilateral kindred rather than patrilocal bands appears to be the solution of choice.

Athapaskan Adaptations illuminates this relatively obscure area of the world and brings it, and the cultures it supported, into the context of modern anthropological theory.

Walter Goldschmidt

Preface

The intent of this study is to describe the ethnography of northern Athapaskans adequately for the beginning student, whether undergraduate or graduate. The book does not pretend to be more than an introduction to what I firmly believe, although with admitted prejudice, to be the most interesting hunters and gatherers on the North American continent. In keeping with the orientation of other volumes in the Worlds of Man series, general patterns are described at the expense of extensive ethnographic detail in the hope that the student will acquire a broad framework and, at the same time, an appreciation for the varieties of adaptations that have enabled northern Athapaskans to survive in their extensive and varied geographic environment. More ethnographic detail can be obtained from the monographs and articles listed in the references and suggested further readings at the end of the book. Consideration is also given to the effects of European contact, particularly the fur trade, which have been the prime factor underlying the culture patterns of contemporary northern Athapaskans.

In order to generalize about the various northern Athapaskan groups, it has been necessary to rely heavily on the work of others. This study owes a considerable intellectual debt to the writings of the pioneer students of northern Athapaskan culture: June Helm, John Honigmann, Diamond Jenness, Catherine McClellan, Robert McKennan, Cornelius Osgood, and Richard Slobodin, to name only a few. In particular, I wish to express my gratitude to June Helm, Catherine McClellan, and Robert Mc-

Kennan who offered valuable suggestions at various stages in the development of this book, and to whose published writings I am more than ordinarily indebted. The manuscript was typed by Lenore Slenczka and Eva A. Ziemba with accuracy and dispatch. The maps were drawn by Zbigniew T. Jastrzebski and Patricia J. Brew.

At various stages of preparation, these pages have been read with thoroughness and thought by Alexander J. Morin of Aldine Publishing Co., and Walter Goldschmidt, editor of the Worlds of Man series. To both of them, my sincere thanks.

Finally, I wish to express appreciation to my wife, Mary Helms VanStone, whose enthusiasm, encouragement, patience, and sympathy, not necessarily in that order, have endured through several drafts of the manuscript. It is to her that the final result is dedicated.

Contents

Foreword   vii

Preface   ix

Introduction   1

1. The Natural Environment and Human Populations   7

2. The Subsistence Base and Settlement Patterns   23

3. Social Institutions   43

4. Religion and the Supernatural   59

5. The Individual and His Culture   74

6. The History of European Contact   90

7. Northern Athapaskans and the Modern World   105

8. Athapaskan Adaptive Strategy   121

Appendix: The Ethnographic Literature and
Future Research Needs   127

Selected References   135

Suggested Further Reading   138

Index   141

Photographs—between pages 58 and 59

INTRODUCTION

The University of Alaska near Fairbanks is located at the edge of a bluff overlooking the Chena River, a tributary of the Tanana, itself an important tributary of the great Yukon River. Although today the University community is part of the greater Fairbanks metropolitan area in central Alaska, traditionally the region was occupied by the Tanana, one of the groups of northern Athapaskan Indians who inhabit interior Alaska and the adjacent northwestern parts of Canada. At the present time, there are many Athapaskan Indians living in the Fairbanks area, but the Tanana can no longer be said to occupy their traditional territory, nor to practice their traditional way of life.

In the fall of 1951, following completion of my graduate studies, I joined the faculty of the Department of Anthropology at the University of Alaska. Like most newcomers to the north, my strongest impressions during that first year centered around the long nights and bone-chilling cold of an interior Alaskan winter. The preceding year, as a graduate student with research interests in the arctic and subarctic, I had enrolled in a course dealing with circumpolar peoples and had learned that although winters in the arctic interior were long and bitter, and absolute temperatures were nearly as low as anywhere in the world, the region lacked the gales and high humidity of the arctic coast. Therefore, living conditions were easier than along the coast where strong winds combined with dampness and extreme cold required Eskimos to wear highly specialized fur clothing and live in solidly constructed underground dwellings.

Although the logic of these facts was unassailable, it was difficult for me to believe, during that first winter in interior Alaska, that any aboriginal people in the world lived under more severe climatic conditions than the Indians of the Tanana valley. On a typical cold, dark, January morning, as I made my way across the campus to an eight o'clock class, the thermometer would stand at −45 or −50 degrees with a thick, dank ice fog settled heavily in the valley. On such days it did not require a great deal of effort to imagine the members of a Tanana Indian family rising stiffly from bed in their skin-covered dwelling, laboriously making a fire to prepare food, and then venturing forth on snowshoes or by dog team through the deep snow in pursuit of scarce game animals. From the warmth and comfort of an overheated classroom, no way of life anywhere seemed to me more difficult or fraught with discouragement.

Since my early years at the University of Alaska, I have spent much time among northern peoples. I have experienced the cold, windy expanses of the arctic coast and, in an approximation of the life of the hypothetical Indian family of my early imagination, I have risen on a cold January morning in a small, unheated tent in the wooded interior of Alaska and the Northwest Territories of Canada. These experiences have taught me that my early notions of northern Athapaskan life were, to say the least, much too simple. Those naive views changed in direct proportion to the increase in my experience and knowledge of the way man adapts to the environments in which he finds himself.

Of the various professional activities that helped me become aware of the complexities of environmental adaptation, perhaps the most significant for the purposes of this account was my field work among Chipewyan Indians living along the east shore of Great Slave Lake in the Northwest Territories. Beginning in the summer of 1960, I worked and lived with these Indians, members of the most eastern group of northern Athapaskans, for a period of eleven months spread over three years. Most of this time was spent in the community of Snowdrift at the northeast end of the lake, a small community where the Indians live for much of the year in a manner quite different from their lifeways prior to European contact. However, I also made several extended trips by snowshoe and dog team with Indian trappers, thereby experiencing at first hand a more traditional way of life with which most northern Athapaskans have been associated for nearly 250 years.

I quickly learned that the inhabitants of this seemingly inhospitable region of northwestern Canada had developed a set of very special adaptations that permeated virtually every aspect of their life. This applied not only to their life prior to European contact in the late eighteenth century, but also to the adjustments they made in response to external pressures of the contact period. These adaptations have enabled them to live successfully in a demanding environment within the framework of a rapidly changing world, and to fill most of their needs by means of acquired skills and with an ease born of long experience. It is true, of course, that like most native North Americans in the 1960s, the Snowdrift Chipewyan had experienced difficulties in adjusting to a changing world that no amount of adaptation to the natural environment could possibly have alleviated. Nevertheless, the source of these difficulties, western civilization, can itself be considered an aspect of the changing environment to which the Snowdrift Indians are in the process of adapting.

The relationship of people to the natural environment has been a major theme of many writers discussing northern peoples, both Eskimos and Athapaskans. This is reasonable since the relationship of hunting and gathering peoples to their physical environment is very direct: they depend exclusively on wild plants and animals for their food, and even the most casual observer can readily note the importance of subsistence activities in their way of life. I have already noted that northern Athapaskans did not experience the extreme pressures from the natural environment that are normally associated with coastal Eskimos. In particular, the physical dangers and difficulties that must be faced in a sea ice environment were unknown to them. In compensation, however, the coastal Eskimos profited from a plentiful supply of sea mammals, and their natural environment must be considered richer than the subarctic interior where large game animals are frequently scarce and only fish are predictably abundant.

The area occupied by northern Athapaskan Indians lies directly south of the true arctic regions in a belt of coniferous forest broken in places by high mountains and stretches of treeless tundra. This great forested area is transcontinental, stretching from Newfoundland to western Alaska. Except in the far western portion where the Rocky Mountains occur, much of this area is of relatively slight elevation, and there are numerous low, rolling, glaciated hills. The climate of the region is characterized by very long, cold winters and short, warm summers. Snowfall is heavier than along the arctic coast, and in general the climate is quite different from the desert-like coastal areas inhabited by Eskimos. The northern Athapaskans inhabit the western part of this coniferous forest belt, specifically the drainage of the Yukon River to the point just short of where it empties into the Bering Sea, and those parts of the Northwest Territories, northern British Columbia, Alberta, Saskatchewan, and Manitoba drained by the Mackenzie River. The total area of Athapaskan occupancy falls naturally into two sections, a Pacific and an arctic drainage area. In spite of the pervasiveness of the northern coniferous forest and its seeming uniformity over vast distances, the mountainous nature of much of the region occupied by northern Athapaskans and its considerable spread—from north to south as well as from east to west—is such that there are few areas of North America within which the environmental contrasts are so great and the natural barriers between native groups so formidable.

The various groups of northern Athapaskans speak languages that belong to the Athapaskan branch of the Na-Dene speech family. In fact, it is primarily language (together with occupation of a common territory) that serves to set off the various Athapaskan groups from one another since, like the Eskimos, they do not have formal tribal organization.

The Na-Dene speech family is the most widespread linguistic phylum in aboriginal North America. It includes the entire Athapaskan family, which in turn is divided into three subfamilies: northern Athapaskan, Pacific Athapaskan, and Apachean. The northern Athapaskan subfamily includes all the different peoples discussed in this book who live in western Canada and interior Alaska. The Pacific Athapaskans are a group of thirteen tribes concentrated in the Pacific Northwest, but extending down into northern California. The best known Apachean speakers are the Apache and Navajo of the American southwest.

On the basis of archaeological evidence, it appears that the ancestral Na-Dene had moved across Bering Strait into what is now Alaska by the tenth millenium B.C. near the end of the final great glacial period. As deglaciation occurred, they spread east and south through the Yukon Territory and interior British Columbia, reaching the present state of Washington by about 4500 B.C.

The environment that is postulated for the initial appearance of the Na-Dene ancestors is treeless tundra. By 8000 to 6000 B.C., however, most of central Alaska was covered with spruce forests, while the corridor leading to British Columbia between the Coast Mountains and the Rocky Mountains was characterized in postglacial times by pine forests. The faunal population of this vast boreal forest area included moose and caribou as well as a variety of small game and fish. Thus the Na-Dene were formed in and became adapted to a subarctic forest environment not greatly different from the one they occupy today.

Students of linguistic history believe that the Na-Dene stock as late as approximately 700 B.C. consisted of a single closely-related group of Indians with its homeland in east central Alaska and possibly a portion of the adjacent Yukon Territory. Dispersal then began to take place and the Pacific Athapaskan subfamily appears to have completed its diversification by about 1000 A.D. At about this time, the Apachean subfamily began moving south, and between 900 and 1400 A.D. diversification within the northern Athapaskan subfamily itself took place.

As the various subfamilies of Athapaskans dispersed south, they were influenced greatly by the cultures of the people with whom they came in contact. This occurred partly because of necessity in new geographical environments and, presumably, partly by choice. The end result of all this culture change was three distinct types of culture so different that without linguistic evidence their common origins never would have been suspected. Scholars have concluded from their study of Athapaskan languages that language is much more stable than other aspects of culture.

One of the most difficult and persistent problems that has faced students of northern Athapaskan culture is the precise definition of the various groups belonging to the language family. Much of this difficulty can be attributed to changes in habitat, occasional invasions of each other's lands, and group mixtures that took place for a variety of reasons. Northern Athapaskans were also highly susceptible to external influences. Thus we find some groups whose cultures closely resemble those of peoples native to the intermountain plateau, while groups located close to the northwest coast have been influenced considerably by the strong cultural impulses emanating from that vigorous area. Athapaskans in the lower Yukon area and in the vicinity of Cook Inlet have borrowed heavily from the Eskimos. Still others, pushing south and west into the prairie, have adopted many traits from the plains area. Thus, when the northern Athapaskan region is considered as a whole, it is necessary to recognize that there are groups living on the fringes whose cultures have been considerably modified, along with those "core groups" which presumably represent a more or less unmodified interior Athapaskan culture. At the same time, we will be well advised to bear in mind that traits that appear to occur as the result of simple diffusion may, in fact, be part of a common cultural base of some antiquity.

Throughout the first five chapters of this book, except where specifically noted, I will be discussing northern Athapaskan culture as it existed prior to first contact with Europeans. In other words, these chapters concern the so-called "ethnographic present," a time no longer remembered in any detail by the Indians themselves, but which can be reconstructed with reasonable accuracy (though with definite limitations) through reference to historical accounts and earlier ethnographic studies. The historic period begins in the eastern Athapaskan area as early as the mid-eighteenth century, while for the extreme northwestern groups, initial contact with Europeans did not take place until nearly 100 years later. Although the present tense may be used occasionally in the early chapters of this book, the reader should remember that it refers to the ethnographic present rather than the actual present.

Chapter 1

THE NATURAL ENVIRONMENT AND HUMAN POPULATIONS

In the past, attempts by scholars to classify northern Athapaskan cultural groups have centered around their arrangement into two major alignments: those of the Arctic and Pacific drainages. The great curving mountain chain of northwestern Canada and central Alaska, an extension of the Rocky Mountains, has served as the dividing line. This basic division emphasized the importance of salmon in the economy of the Indians: the Athapaskan groups in the Pacific drainage west of the mountains relied heavily on salmon, while those in the arctic drainage to the east lacked this important food source.

In recent years many specialists have questioned this emphasis on the role of salmon and a corresponding lack of attention to the importance of various land animals, particularly caribou, moose, and sheep. As a result, various attempts have been made to set up a more detailed regional classification, one that stresses the significance of the mountainous habitat of many of these people. Behind this emphasis is the idea that northern Athapaskans can best be understood as basically a mountain people who have, in some cases, moved out of the cordilleran area. This approach stresses the great ecological contrasts within northwestern North America and the flexibility of Athapaskan culture in general, a flexibility that is also illustrated by their susceptibility to external influences.

Before considering the natural environment and related spatial distribution of northern Athapaskans, it is useful to discuss the extent to which the term "tribe" can be applied to groups, none of which formed distinct political units. There was no tribal organization and, among most groups, only a very limited tribal consciousness. Northern Athapaskan culture has been described as consisting not of a series of neat cultural entities, but as a cultural continuum carried on by a series of interlocking groups whose individual lifeways differed only in certain minor details from those of their immediate neighbors. Such minor variations were observable only when they had built up into more significant differences, usually over considerable geographical distance. Thus the cultures of Athapaskan groups inhabiting the lower and middle Yukon River region were very similar, but quite noticeably different from those of the upper Mackenzie valley. What have sometimes been called tribes were, therefore, simply spatially localized groups, distinguished for the most part by relatively slight cultural differences.

What was true for culture was apparently also true of language, although published studies are lacking. One researcher has noted that when he asked his informants about differences in the dialects of the various local groups being studied, he was invariably told that the neighboring Indians spoke "just the same as us, only a little bit different." Doubtless this was true of much of the Athapaskan area, linguistic differences increasing with distance until the dialects were no longer mutually intelligible.

In dealing with the various Athapaskan groups, anthropologists have invariably found it necessary to consider the problem of determining suitable names. The literature is full of names given to specific groups of Indians by travelers, explorers, missionaries and others. The Tanana Indians, for example, are known by no less than six names. All these terms, although bestowed upon the Tanana by visiting white men, represent names by which other Indian people have designated the inhabitants of the Tanana drainage. Virtually all the names by which we conventionally refer to the various Athapaskan groups, and which are used in this chapter, are simply descriptive names used by one people to refer to the members of a foreign group. The inhabitants of a particular area within the Athapaskan region were likely to refer to themselves as "Dene," meaning "people." Descriptive terms were invariably reserved for more distant neighbors.

The depiction of the distribution of northern Athapaskans on a map is certain to introduce a kind of rigidity that tends to negate many of the points about cultural and linguistic flexibility just mentioned. Therefore, it should be kept in mind that the boundaries indicated on the map on p. 10 are very approximate and show only in a general way the limits to which members of a particular group might extend their activities and the maximum area utilized at any given time in the group's history. The subtle linguistic and cultural overlappings that have occurred throughout the region cannot be indicated on such a map. For example, it is known that the Ingalik Indians living along the lower Innoko River, a major tributary of the Yukon, frequently hunted for caribou in the higher country of the upper river, which is well within the territory shown on the map as having been occupied by the closely-related Koyukon group. Despite its shortcomings, the map gives a general, comparative picture of Athapaskan distributions and can be useful if these reservations are kept continually in mind.

Let us now consider five contiguous physiographic units into which the total area occupied by northern Athapaskans can conveniently be divided. Such a division, first suggested by Catherine McClellan (1970), gives maximum recognition to the most significant ecological factors that have influenced the lives of the Indians.

ARCTIC DRAINAGE LOWLANDS

This region, dominated by the basin of the Mackenzie River, is the habitat of those people who occupy the western Canadian shield from northern Manitoba, Alberta, and Saskatchewan west and northwest through Great Slave Lake and Great Bear Lake to latitude timberline as it extends from the vicinity of Hudson Bay to the Mackenzie River. The topography is characterized by a plateau base in excess of 1500 feet from which higher elevations rise repeatedly in patterns that include lakes and connecting rivers. In fact, throughout much of this area,

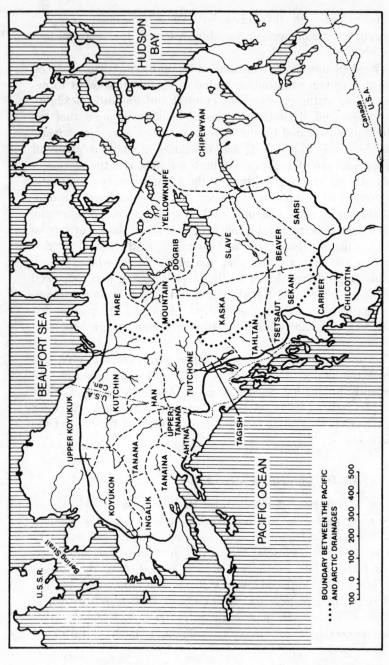

Figure 1. Distribution of northern Athapaskan Indians (modified from Osgood, 1936b with permission of the Human

Map labels:

HUDSON BAY

BEAUFORT SEA

PACIFIC OCEAN

U.S.S.R.

Bering Strait

Canada / U.S.A.

CHIPEWYAN
YELLOWKNIFE
DOGRIB
MOUNTAIN
HARE
SLAVE
KASKA
SEKANI
BEAVER
SARSI
CARRIER
CHILCOTIN
TAHLTAN
TSETSAUT
TUTCHONE
KUTCHIN
HAN
UPPER TANANA
AHTNA
TANAINA
TANANA
KOYUKON
INGALIK
UPPER KOYUKUK
TAGISH
U.S.A. / Can.

BOUNDARY BETWEEN THE PACIFIC
AND ARCTIC DRAINAGES

100   0   100   200   300   400   500

Table 1. Northern Athapaskan Populations*

Arctic Drainage Lowlands	Cordilleran
Hare 420 (1867)	Upper Koyukuk 300 (1885)
Bear Lake ?	Kutchin 1200 (1860)
Dogrib 788 (1864)	Mountain 250 (1906)
Yellowknife 220 (1859)	Han 500 (1875)
Chipewyan 2420 (1906)	Upper Tanana 152 (1930)
Slave 850 (1906)	Tutchone 1110 (1900)
Beaver 380 (1914)	Tagish 100 (1944)
Sarsi 450 (1880)	Kaska 300 (1850)
	Tahltan 229 (1909)
Yukon and Kuskokwim River Basins	Tsetsaut 500 (1830)
Ingalik 2000 (1870)	Sekani 500 (1890)
Koyukon 940 (1890)	Carrier 876 (1906)
Tanana 550 (1887)	Chilcotin 450 (1906)
Cook Inlet-Susitna River Basin	Copper River Basin
Tanaina 739 (1880)	Atna 366 (1887)

*Population figures given here are, in all but a few cases, the most reliable available for the late 19th and early 20th centuries. By this date, however, many Athapaskan populations had been badly decimated by epidemics of European diseases.

water occupies a quarter to a third of the landscape. In some places the Pre-Cambrian bedrock has been exposed by glaciation, but over most areas, extensive glacial deposits occur.

The climate of this vast area is continental and relatively uniform. Winters are long and severe, usually continually below freezing, but summers can be quite warm considering the northern latitude. In summer there is frequently a considerable variation in temperature within a twenty-four hour period. For example, at Fort Good Hope on July 27, 1958, the maximum temperature was 83° F and the minimum 40° F. Winter months are normally quite severe. In the Mackenzie basin the daily mean temperatures for December, January, and February, based on observations over a thirty-two year period, were −12°, −18°, and −11° F respectively. Temperatures of from −40° to −60° F were not unusual during these months. Throughout most of the area snow is on the ground from October until April or early May. Great Slave Lake freezes in early November and is

Map of the Eastern Athapaskan Area.

Map of the Western Athapaskan Area.

13

usually not clear of ice until the middle of June. The Mackenzie River usually freezes during the first half of November and breakup occurs in late May. It is only in the extreme southwestern section of the Arctic drainage lowlands that this continental climate is slightly tempered by traces of the warm Pacific coast winds, the "Chinook," blowing through the mountain passes.

Vegetation in the arctic drainage lowlands is predominantly coniferous, white spruce being most important and pine virtually absent. In the better drained areas, poplar stands are characteristic and in swampy sections black spruce, tamarak, willow, and alder are abundant. At the eastern borders of the region the trees are small, large stands being limited to sheltered valleys. Ground cover throughout the entire area is heavy. Grass grows in the vicinity of human settlements and on other cleared areas. Blueberries, cranberries, strawberries, and other edible berries are plentiful. In most of the area during early summer wild roses, fireweed, Labrador tea, and other common subarctic flora bloom in profusion.

The fauna of the region does not differ in any marked respect from the rest of northwestern Canada. Animals of economic significance to the Indians include moose, caribou, black and brown bear, foxes of various species, muskrat, beaver, porcupine, hare, marten, lynx, wolverine, otter, fisher, wolf, and red squirrel. Fishing is, of course, an important subsistence activity and the fish most commonly taken are whitefish, grayling, northern pike, lake trout, inconnu (sheefish), suckers, and loche (burbot). Large numbers of ducks and geese appear seasonally and loons are very common.

Eight groups of Indians inhabit the Arctic drainage lowlands, the best known being the Chipewyan, Dogrib, and Slave. The Chipewyan were the most widely spread of all northern Athapaskans, and indeed, their territory was larger than that of any other single North American Indian group. Today, however, much of their vast area is neither occupied nor utilized. The Slave and Chipewyan experienced early contact with European traders and the consequent availability of firearms greatly influenced their relations with each other and with their neighbors.

Closely related to the Chipewyan were the Yellowknife, now extinct and not even remembered as a distinct group by present inhabitants of the general region. In recent years much of their area has been exploited by the Dogrib, and it is possible that the Yellowknife disappeared through merging with both Dogrib and Chipewyan.

Marginal to the Arctic drainage lowlands because of their extreme southern location are the Beaver and Sarsi (Sarcee) Indians. Unlike most other northern Athapaskans, both groups have been largely displaced from their aboriginal territory by European settlement. Today they are to be found on reservations in northern and central Alberta. Although Athapaskan-speaking, the Sarsi have a plains culture as a result of close relations with the Blackfoot.

CORDILLERAN

The second physiographic unit is named in recognition of the great mountain chain that runs in a generally south to north direction through western British Columbia and the Yukon Territory into Alaska. The Coast Mountains, which include the Alaska Range, must be considered a significant physiographic subprovince of the cordilleran region because they exert considerable influence on the climate of the subarctic interior.

Some of the Athapaskan groups that occupy the southern section of the cordilleran region extend eastward into an area of western Canada frequently referred to as "the interior plains." This region is a northward extension of the Great Plains section of southern Alberta, Saskatchewan, and southwestern Manitoba.

Virtually all the cordilleran region is within the circumpolar boreal forest belt and thus the flora throughout much of the area is similar to that already described for the Arctic drainage lowlands. A particularly lush vegetation is found in the lower valley of the Stikine River where a more moderate climate and heavy rainfall have resulted in luxuriant forests of spruce, fir, cedar, and hemlock on the mountain slopes, and groves of large cottonwoods together with impenetrable alder and willow growth in the river and stream valleys. In the northern sections of the cordilleran region, altitude timberline ranges from 2000 to 2500 feet, sometimes a little higher along major rivers and streams. Therefore, much of the piedmont and alpine areas utilized by Indians in these regions are without timber. The Yukon and Mackenzie flats are thickly timbered, primarily with spruce, larch, cotton-woods, and willows.

Climate throughout the cordilleran region is rather dry and somewhat more varied than the vegetation. Most of the moisture falls during the winter months as snow. The lower Stikine River region is again an exception with high humidity and an annual precipitation in the neighborhood of 85 inches. Throughout most of the cordilleran region the winters are extremely cold with temperatures frequently falling below −50° F. Humidity is generally low and practically all bodies of water except the fastest streams are frozen. Summers, in contrast, are extremely hot with temperatures frequently reaching 80° and even 90° F. Frosts occur around the middle of August and intermittent snowfall can be expected after the first of September, reaching a depth of three or four feet by the end of January. By late October and sometimes earlier in high country, rivers run with slush, small lakes and sloughs are frozen, and ice begins to form along the shores of the larger, faster streams. Early in March, the powdery snow of winter forms a thick crust as the sun becomes warmer. Spring breakup occurs at about the same time as in the arctic drainage lowlands region.

It is perhaps pertinent to mention here that throughout the entire region occupied by northern Athapaskans, the days are extremely long in summer and short in winter. In the vicinity of latitude 60° N, which runs through the center of Athapaskan territory, by late June or early July the sun rises at approximately 2:30 a.m. and sets at about 10:30 p.m. At this time, complete darkness is absent. In December the sun rises at about 9:30 a.m. and sets about 3:00 p.m. During the winter, the sun is always low on the horizon and does not give off much heat.

Rivers throughout much of the cordilleran region, except in the extreme southern and northwestern areas, drain eastward and northwest to the Arctic. As a result, the Indian inhabitants lacked the great runs of salmon that are characteristic of the Pacific drainage area. Trout and whitefish, however, are abundant in the region. In the forested areas black and grizzly bears, moose, beaver, and other furbearers, porcupine, hare, and other small animals characteristic of the American northwest are relatively common. On the mountain slopes caribou, goats, and sheep are found. In the southeastern part of the cordilleran region, which reaches out to include the prairies south of the Peace River, there were vast herds of buffalo. Ptarmigan are numerous and economically important throughout much of the area, and in spring and fall there are extensive flocks of waterfowl about the lakes and streams.

A characteristic and unpleasant feature of most of the interior northwest is the clouds of mosquitoes that appear as soon as the snow begins to melt in the spring and last until at least the middle of August. They are replaced by the equally annoying "no-see-um," a small fly that remains active until late in October. Many observers, past and present, have noted that the summer insect life of the Athapaskan area is a far greater source of unpleasantness than the cold, deep snow and long nights of winter.

The fact that thirteen groups of Indians live within the cordilleran region emphasizes the significance of this environmental unit. The most westerly group is the Upper Koyukuk Indians, often considered a part of the Koyukon. These riverine people occupy the area between the upper Koyukuk and the upper Kobuk rivers and have been in close contact with Eskimo inhabitants of the latter region at least since 1850. Their subsistence depends more on large upland game animals than does that of the Koyukon Indians. The Upper Tanana are also distinguished as a separate group, although in fact they are simply those Indians who occupy the mountainous section of the total Tanana territory.

In addition to the Upper Koyukuk Indians, a number of other cordilleran groups have been strongly influenced by their neighbors. The Tutchone and Tagish have borrowed many cultural traits from the nearby coastal Tlingit, the Tagish even preferring to speak that language. The Tsetsaut have been heavily influenced by another northwest coast group, the Tsimshian, while the Carrier and Chilcotin to the extreme south are within the plateau cultural sphere.

YUKON AND KUSKOKWIM RIVER BASINS

The three remaining physiographic units fall entirely within Alaska and thus are inhabited by the most western groups of northern Athapaskans. The first of these, the Yukon and Kuskokwim river basins, is really two extensive lowland areas formed by the valleys of the two great rivers. Included is the valley of the Yukon from the mouth of one of its major tributaries, the Tanana, to the vicinity of the community of Holy Cross, a village which marks the approximate boundary of Athapaskan-speaking people on the river. Below this point on the Yukon, and throughout the vast delta region, the native inhabitants are Eskimos. The valley of the Kuskokwim is also included from its headwaters in the vicinity of Lake Minchumina to the village of Sleetmiut, the approximate Athapaskan boundary prior to European contact. Both the Yukon and Kuskokwim have numerous and sizeable tributaries, and these watercourses naturally have played a dominant role in the life of the Indians who live in the region.

The climate of the Yukon and Kuskokwim river basins varies, the higher country being extremely cold in winter, whereas the lowlands, for the most part, have the most moderate weather in interior Alaska and a considerable amount of rainfall in summer. The region as a whole is well-timbered with heavy spruce forests particularly along the river banks. There are some areas of tundra and swamp as well as barren country. Tamarak is abundant in the swampy areas and thickets of alders are particularly common from the shores of streams and creeks to the vicinity of timberline at about 2500 feet.

The animal life of the region is typical of that found throughout much of interior Alaska. There are bears, moose, and caribou as well as most of the furbearing animals already mentioned. Several varieties of salmon make spawning runs into the Yukon, the Kuskokwim, and their tributaries. Other fresh water fish also occur including whitefish, pike, ling, blackfish and grayling. Most of the birds are migratory, including ducks and geese which nest by the thousands in the Yukon Delta. The annoying mosquitoes and other insects occur in even greater numbers and for longer periods of time here than elsewhere in the north.

There are three groups of Athapaskan Indians living in the Yukon and Kuskokwim river basins: the Ingalik, Tanana, and Koyukon. The Ingalik are perhaps the best known Athapaskan group ethnographically, and because of their proximity to the Eskimos, they have been influenced by these people to a greater extent than any other group.

COOK INLET-SUSITNA RIVER BASIN

Cook Inlet, which dominates this physiographic unit, is one of the deepest indentations of the west coast of North America and is noted as an area of extreme tidal variation, second only to the Bay of Fundy in Nova Scotia. In general, the coastal contours of this region are low, but inland the snow-capped mountains of the Alaska Range rise to a height of more than 10,000 feet, while the Kenai Peninsula is characterized by the Kenai Mountains, with their rugged foothills and tableland. West of the Alaska Range is Iliamna Lake, the largest in Alaska. The Athapaskan-Eskimo boundary runs through this lake, roughly the lower half being occupied by Eskimos. A wide gravel plain extends northwest from the head of Cook Inlet, and the broad flats of the lower Susitna River form the region's northern boundary.

As might be expected in an area of extreme topographic differentiation, the climate of the Cook Inlet-Susitna River basin shows considerable variation. The lower inlet has a moderate climate tempered by the Japan Current; the upper inlet country is colder, but the climate is still tempered to some extent by the nearness of the sea. Environmentally, the area surrounding the Susitna River valley is more closely related to the interior Athapaskan country already described because of the extreme winter cold. Vegetation in the Cook Inlet-Susitna River basin area is less variable than the climate. Spruce covers the lowlands and the lower slopes of the mountains and there are groves of birch and cottonwood in some locations; extensive grasslands are characteristic of the upper inlet, and typical tundra vegetation is to be found in the vicinity of Iliamna Lake.

Fish and land animals are plentiful in the Cook Inlet-Susitna River basin. Salmon appear seasonally in the Susitna and its tributaries as well as in all other rivers flowing into Cook Inlet. Moose are more abundant here than in most other parts of the northern Athapaskan region. Caribou are found in the upper inlet, while bears, beaver, porcupine, hare, wolverine, lynx, and muskrat are common throughout the entire area. Mountain sheep and mountain goats have a limited range, but nevertheless contribute significantly to the food supply of the native inhabitants. Migratory waterfowl are common from April to October and ptarmigan are also seasonal, at least as far as hunting is concerned, since they move to inaccessible mountain country during the summer.

The Tanaina Indians, the only northern Athapaskans who live along the sea coast, occupy the Cook Inlet-Susitna River basin. Hence, sea mammals are of considerable subsistence importance, and Eskimo cultural influence is strong. The hair and fur seal, the sea otter, sea lion, porpoise, and beluga (white whale) were all hunted. Sea mammals are more plentiful in the lower reaches of Cook Inlet, only the hair seal and beluga being common in the upper inlet, and then only when there is open water.

COPPER RIVER BASIN

One of the most rugged areas inhabited by Athapaskans in Alaska is the Copper River basin. The river, which has the steepest gradient of any major waterway in Alaska, heads in the Alaska Range, and its valley cuts through lofty mountain passes, rolling uplands, and wide plains on its way to the sea. The surface of the basin, into which the Copper River and its tributaries have cut their valleys, is a poorly drained, swampy area with many lakes, which supports only a scanty vegetation of stunted spruce and moss. The valley bottom and slopes, however, have a luxuriant growth of spruce, some birch, aspen, poplar, alder, and willows. The climate of this wild region is similar to that of the Susitna River basin, although precipitation tends to be somewhat greater. Salmon run in abundance in the Copper River and the game and furbearing animals, except for sea mammals, are similar to those of the Cook Inlet region. This rich and varied area is occupied by the Atna who, at the mouth of the river, are in contact with the nearly extinct Eyak, an Athapaskan-related people showing strong northwest coast influences.

ECOLOGICAL CHANGES

My description of the distribution of flora and fauna in the regions occupied by northern Athapaskans are of necessity very general, and do not do justice to the ecological variations that are found in each of the physiographic units described. Moose, for example, are generally confined to broad river valleys and lower altitudes where browse is plentiful. Caribou are more widely distributed, but are nevertheless primarily upland animals and inhabit the mountainous headwaters of rivers. These ecological variations are significant in terms of the seasonal movements of peoples in any given area.

It should also be emphasized that the distribution of flora and fauna as outlined here is essentially the situation as it exists at the present time. There are reasons to believe that distributions may have been different in the early historic period and that the environment has changed significantly over the past century and a half. Unfortunately for the purposes of this book, these changes have not been documented in detail, and it is only in a few areas that we can glimpse the process of change as it has taken place.

It is generally believed that moose are now more common in the region occupied by northern Athapaskans than they were half a century ago. Information on this subject is usually obtained by anthropologists from Indian informants and is difficult to verify. The Upper Tanana Indians believe that these animals appeared in the Chandalar River region within the past two generations and that for some years after their appearance, there was a taboo against killing them. A Tanaina Indian described seeing his first moose in the Kachemak Bay area of Cook Inlet in the 1880s while hunting with his brother: both boys rushed back to the camp believing they had seen a white man's horse. On the other hand, some experienced forest ecologists doubt that moose are recent migrants into any part of Alaska.

Native traditions also frequently refer to changes in the flora. At some unspecified time in the past, spruce are said to have been largely absent from the Yukon Flats, which were then covered with willows. More accurate data than that provided by native traditions are required to demonstrate that significant changes in regional ecology have occurred in any given area, but such traditions can provide interesting leads. During the mid-nineteenth century, for example, moose are said to have been abundant in the vicinity of the Hudson Bay Company post at Fort Yukon, a fact that was doubtless related to the absence of spruce and birch in the region and the abundance of willows on which the animals browse. There is considerable evidence that moose have gradually been spreading into the tundra north of the Yukon River and this movement has been associated with the extension of tall willows into this area. This, in turn, may be connected with the gradual holarctic warming that appears to have taken place. Such evidence, lends weight to statements made by Indian informants about changes in flora and fauna of the area, and their belief that winters have been becoming gradually milder.

Obviously, more scientific data on the climate, flora, and fauna of the Athapaskan area is needed before definite statements concerning ecological change can be made and substantiated and the statements of Indian informants accurately evaluated. Even without such scientific data, however, it can be stated with certainty that there have been significant environmental changes throughout the entire region in the last 150 years. Any discussion of human ecology in any part of the boreal forest biome should take into consideration fluctuations in resource availability and their significance.

Boreas

biometry : collect calculations of the probable duration of human life.

Chapter 2

THE SUBSISTENCE BASE
AND SETTLEMENT PATTERNS

SUBSISTENCE PATTERNS

In considering Athapaskan subsistence and settlement patterns, which provide the foundations for social life and are closely related to social behavior and institutions, I will stress the adaptations on which survival depends. This is an important and indeed almost inevitable emphasis because of the relatively severe natural environment throughout the western subarctic. It has been noted that this environment is less severe in some ways than that occupied by Eskimos, doubtless one of the reasons why Athapaskans have never been considered as ingenious in their adaptations as the Eskimo. Nevertheless, the northern Athapaskans not only have made many specialized adaptations to the environment in which they live, but have exhibited considerable flexibility in their response to conditions within their total environment and to cultural impulses from neighboring peoples.

The subsistence activities of all northern Athapaskans, like those of most of the world's peoples, reflected a changing economic relationship to their environment in the course of the year. Athapaskans were exclusively hunters and gatherers, but there were considerable differences in emphasis in the use by specific groups of the natural resources available to them. Most of these differences involved stressing either hunting or fishing. In this section we will discuss the subsistence of representative groups within the various physiographic subdivisions inhabited by northern Athapaskans with particular emphasis on the baseline adaptation to interior or subarctic conditions. Some consideration will be given, however, to adaptations by those groups that live at the fringes of the Athapaskan area.

The Indians of the Arctic drainage lowlands were primarily hunters, exploiting all the animal resources available in their environment. Typical of these interior hunters were the Chipewyan, who were particularly dependent on the caribou as the chief source of their food. Geographically, the Chipewyan were in a position to utilize both the Barren Ground and the Woodland caribou. Unlike other large northern game animals, caribou gather in herds that migrate hundreds of miles in search of food and in response to seasonal changes: Barren Ground caribou, for example, move to the tundra in spring and come back to the edge of the forests in late fall. Caribou drives took place mainly in the late fall or early winter in open country. Two long, converging rows of wooden sticks were set up leading to a large enclosure of branches. Snares of babiche (semi-tanned caribou or moose hide) were set in the enclosure and when the animals followed along the converging row of sticks, they found themselves in the enclosure and caught in snares. There they could be killed easily by the hunters with bows and arrows (see illustrations).* Water drives were also employed, the animals being lanced or stabbed with knives from canoes once they had been driven into a lake where they were helpless. It is worth special note that for all northern Athapaskans, snares, although simple in design and implementation, were extremely effective for taking game and fur animals.

Moose were not particularly important to the Chipewyan, but they were of paramount importance to the Slave who lived to the south of the thick forests. Although common throughout much of the boreal regions of North America, moose are most abundant in second growth birch forests that come in after fires, and along the larger rivers of interior country. They are browsing animals and prefer to feed on the leaves of birch, willow, and aspen trees)

*Illustrations are in the photo section between pp. 58 and 59.

It follows that people like the Chipewyan who inhabit timberline plateaus were primarily caribou hunters, whereas lowland and riverine dwellers like the Slave hunted moose.

Among the Slave, moose were snared and hunted with bows and arrows. Semicircular tracking, a characteristic method of hunting moose in winter, has been described for several Athapaskan groups including the Slave. When a hunter came upon fresh moose tracks in the snow, he followed them by making wide semicircles to leeward until the trail disappeared, indicating that the animal had doubled back before stopping to feed or lie down. The hunter then also doubled back in smaller semicircles until he located the animal. This type of hunting was most successfully pursued by individual hunters or two men hunting together, in marked contrast to the caribou drive, which required the cooperative efforts of many hunters.

Although moose and caribou were major staples, the animal inventory in the arctic drainage lowlands is extensive, and most were utilized to a greater or lesser extent by groups like the Chipewyan and Slave. Among the former, black bears, wolverine, and smaller furbearing animals were caught in deadfalls, shot with bow and arrow, captured in nets of babiche, or taken by the simple expedient of destroying their houses or dens. Snares were set for hare and ptarmigan, both of which were numerous in winter. Aside from moose, beaver and black bear were the principal animals hunted by the Slave. The former were gaffed at all times of the year after being driven from their houses, while bears were usually taken in summer with babiche snares in berry patches.

Fishing seems to have been more important to the Chipewyan than to most of the arctic drainage lowlands Indians. Trout, whitefish, pike, and other species were speared from canoes in lakes or caught in weirs constructed in the shallow areas of rivers. Gill nets were used in summer and, more rarely, in winter under the ice (see illustrations). Fish were also hooked at all times of the year. Like the Chipewyan, the Slave used gill nets and weirs for a variety of fish including pike, jackfish, gold-eye, suckers, and loche. These fish were usually taken in January and February through the ice. Both groups gathered bird eggs and various wild berries, but gathering was not a primary economic activity.

Fishing and hunting small game were always considered important by the Chipewyan and Slave because these activities provided food during periods of scarcity when the principal food animals declined. In the event of extreme need, caribou or moose hunters could always camp by a lake and subsist on the fish obtained through the ice. The snowshoe hare, porcupine, and other small game species, a mere diet supplement in times of plenty, could save lives when food was scarce (see illustrations). It is safe to say that throughout the arctic drainage lowlands, when moose and caribou were available, all other forms of subsistence were distinctly subsidiary. However, the necessity of dealing with periods of game scarcity emphasizes the significance of a phenomenon that is characteristic throughout the boreal forest environment: almost every food resource is subject to fluctuations in abundance, regular or irregular.

During the aboriginal period, all winter hunting was carried out on foot, since dogs were not yet used for pulling sledges or toboggans. Therefore, snowshoes were an important item of material culture and many northern Athapaskans made two types. The first, called hunting snowshoes, were long and rounded in front, and were used for walking over fresh snow. The second type, travel snowshoes, were shorter with a pointed and sharply upturned front end. These smaller snowshoes allowed the wearer to sink more deeply into the snow and were used for walking on a previously broken trail, or, in later times, to break a trail for a dog team.

In the northern part of the cordilleran region subsistence also centered around the hunting of large game animals. The Kutchin, however, extending considerably to the west of the mountain chain, exhibited greater overall diversity in their subsistence activities. The Chandalar Kutchin were typically big game hunters of the high country. Caribou, the most important animals hunted, were taken in surrounds similar to those already described. When large game was scarce, many small mammals provided an alternative food supply, as did a variety of birds, particularly ptarmigan and spruce hens in winter and ducks and geese during the summer months. Both roots and berries were plentiful, but, as in other Athapaskan areas, they cannot be considered an important food source. Unlike other Kutchin, the

Chandalar made little use of fish, although they were occasionally taken in winter through the ice.

This lack of emphasis on fishing tended to separate the Chandalar Kutchin from the groups to the west. In the Yukon Flats area, for example, from early July until early September the Indians fished for salmon, three species (king, dog, silver) of which ascend the river. They were taken with dip nets and basket-shaped traps. When the fishing season was over, the Yukon Flats people hunted moose and caribou until the river was frozen. In winter game was scarce and the Indians were forced to scatter in family groups.

Although predictable fish runs allowed the Yukon Flats Kutchin to enjoy a certain stability unknown to peoples almost completely dependent on hunting, periods of starvation were known to all the Kutchin and, indeed, to most Athapaskans. At such times the Indians have been said to survive by making a broth from animal dung and eating the inner bark of willows. Cannibalism occasionally occurred under such stress, as it did among arctic drainage lowlands peoples.

In the southern cordilleran region the Tahltan, an upland people, practiced aboriginal subsistence activities similar to those of the Chandalar Kutchin. Here the caribou, mountain sheep, and moose were important, particularly the caribou. There is much open country in this region of northern British Columbia and the caribou hunters made use of drives and snares in the late fall and winter when the animals travel in herds. Bears, mountain goats, and mountain sheep also live in the upland environment. Bears were taken with deadfalls and snares, or shot with bow and arrow in their hibernating holes. Goats and sheep had to be stalked individually over the rugged terrain. Toward the coast where game animals are less abundant, fishing took on added importance. However, the lower valley of the Stikine River has never been permanently occupied by either the Tahltan or their neighbors, the Tlingit. Salmon are abundant in the Stikine, but this river and its tributaries are swift streams winding through deep gorges that offer few fishing places. In such water, nets, weirs, and traps are ineffective. Since the waters are muddy, spears are equally useless, and most salmon were taken with gaffs.

When we turn to the Yukon and Kuskokwim river basins and

consider the subsistence activities of the Ingalik, we are in an area where fishing was of primary importance and, in the aboriginal period, took precedence over all other forms of subsistence. The Ingalik hunted caribou, moose, bear, and most of the other subarctic animals previously mentioned, but it was fishing that gave stability to their way of life, a stability not approached in the other physiographic regions we have discussed.

In keeping with the importance of fishing and the variety of fish available in the environment, the Ingalik had a highly developed fishing technology. Long-handled dip nets were used for taking salmon in spring and summer, and net-like drags of willows were satisfactory for use in the shallow waters of the innumerable Yukon sloughs. For lake fishing, fish-shaped lurehooks were characteristic and gill nets of various sizes were used in both summer and winter. It should be remembered that the netting of fish involves a whole complex of net-making equipment including the netting material itself, usually willow bast line, along with shuttles, needles, gauges, weights, and bark floats.

By far the most common method of fishing among the Ingalik, however, was the use of basket-shaped traps made of thin spruce wood sticks lashed together with spruce root line. These traps had funnel-shaped mouths, sometimes made of a separate piece, which tapered to a hole barely large enough for a fish to pass through. The body of the trap was cylindrical and frequently tapered to a point at the end opposite the mouth. Traps of varying sizes and slightly different shapes were set for dog salmon, whitefish, loche, blackfish, jackfish, and grayling. They were set in swift water in spring and summer, and under ice in winter. Frequently traps were associated with fences that directed the fish to the trap, occasionally stretching completely across a small stream or slough. Traps were particularly effective in the muddy waters of the Yukon and its lower tributaries where they could not be seen by the fish (see illustrations).

At the beginning of the twentieth century, fish wheels were introduced by American miners all along the Yukon and rapidly superseded most of the other open water fishing methods. A fish wheel consists of several enclosed paddles that are propelled in circles by the action of the current. The paddles are fixed to a framework anchored along the river bank. As the paddles rotate, fish are caught in them and slide into a live-box fixed to the framework (see illustrations). Like traps, these ingenious fish-taking devices are effective only in rivers and streams with muddy water. They have the advantage of not needing to be checked as frequently as nets or traps.

Most fish caught during summer months were dried and stored in caches for dog food as well as human consumption. Each fish was split along one side of the backbone to the tail and horizontal slices were cut into the meat to allow easier drying. The fish were then hung on a pole-frame drying rack. Slow, smoky fires were built under the hanging fish to keep off flies and to encourage faster drying (see illustrations).

As previously noted, the Tanaina Indians in the Cook Inlet-Susitna River basin area are the only Athapaskans who live on the sea coast. Sea mammal hunting was of considerable importance in restricted areas of their territory. Seals were hunted in Cook Inlet, being frequently taken at low tide when the animals were on the beach. The hunters, swimming in from boats, imitated the movements of the seals and then clubbed the animals after reaching the shore. The Cook Inlet Tanaina also possessed Eskimo-like kayaks, from which seals were hunted with bows and arrows or harpoons.

Sea otters, whose skins were highly prized in the early period of European contact, were hunted by special parties organized for the purpose, usually using several kayaks under the leadership of a hunting chief. The animals could be killed easily with bows and arrows in calm weather when they were sleeping on their backs. They were also taken by means of harpoons with detachable, barbed points of bone or antler.

The hunting of sea lions was restricted to the Kachemak Bay region. These large animals were usually harpooned, the wounded creature dragging a line with a sealskin float attached until it tired and could be killed by the hunter with a bone-headed spear.

The beluga or white whale is, along with the seal, the most widely distributed sea mammal in Tanaina territory. Belugas appear well into the upper inlet area, where they break through the ice during mild winters to feed on tomcod. Several hunters were usually required in taking belugas, and the big animals were hunted with the same size of harpoon used for sea lions.

When the beluga tired from dragging the float, it could be easily approached and killed with a spear.

Even this brief discussion of Tanaina sea mammal hunting should indicate that in these particular activities, the Indians were heavily influenced by their Eskimo neighbors. There were many opportunities for contact between the Tanaina and the Eskimos of southwestern Alaska. Since Eskimos had presumably been in the area considerably longer than the Tanaina, it is probable that they had achieved a more efficient adaptation to the inlet environment. The Tanaina appear to have moved into the southwestern coastal region in late prehistoric times. It is therefore not surprising that they borrowed material culture traits related to coastal activities from the neighboring Eskimo to supplement their otherwise interior-oriented culture.

Although the Tanaina are distinctive because their environment permitted the hunting of sea mammals, large game animals were also important to them. Black bears were particularly numerous in every part of Tanaina country and the Indians killed them at all times of the year, primarily by means of snares and deadfalls. Caribou were hunted with dogs who drove the animals toward the waiting hunters. In the upper inlet region, herds were quite large and the Indians constructed surrounds. Moose were also plentiful in most areas of Tanaina country and were taken by the methods that have already been described. Mountain sheep and mountain goats had a limited range on the eastern edge of the upper inlet country, but hunting expeditions for these animals were frequently arranged and dogs were used in the chase. It is evident that the Tanaina lived in an area rich in game, the environment being similar in many ways to that of the northern cordilleran area, with the addition of sea mammals.

The subsistence patterns of the Atna of the Copper River basin have never been described in detail. Although living in a mountainous region rich in big game, the Atna, like the Yukon and Kuskokwim river basin tribes, depended heavily on salmon fishing. In the turbulent Copper River, fishing presented special problems that did not very often occur elsewhere in the Athapaskan area. Gill nets and traps were easily swept away by the fast water, so the Indians depended heavily on dip nets to take the several varieties of salmon as they ascended the river to spawn. Moose and bear were the most important big game animals, but early explorers in the area reported that the Atna depended heavily on small game, particularly hares, to carry them through those periods in late winter and early spring when supplies of dried fish were low.

In the previous pages, no attempt has been made to describe in detail every subsistence activity of the northern Athapaskan groups, nor to assess the economic importance of every plant and animal in the environment. Rather, my emphasis has been on those activities and techniques that were of particular importance in the major ecological zones of the region. This approach has perhaps obscured the fact that throughout the region there was considerable uniformity. Every animal in the environment was utilized when the need arose, and many of the methods and techniques used to take them were common throughout the area. Subsistence activities in the western subarctic were highly generalized, at least in comparison with the specialized nature of subsistence in some other areas of North America.

Nevertheless, we have noted certain specializations in the various geographical units which make up the total region. In general, big game hunting tended to be more important to those people living at the headwaters of the major rivers and their tributaries and those whose territories encompassed the divide between the Pacific and Arctic drainages. In these areas, particularly where caribou occurred in large numbers, hunting techniques were quite specialized and frequently required the organized effort of a sizeable number of people.

We have also noted that where salmon occurred, they provided a predictable supply of food and were taken with specialized equipment adapted to the various riverine environments of the region. In addition, the presence of these fish made possible a relatively settled way of life that was not possible in areas where people followed the seasonal movements of large game animals.

Writers attempting to generalize about northern Athapaskan culture have frequently cited these subsistence patterns and food shortages as evidence for marginality and cultural impoverishment. While it is undeniable that periods of food scarcity are known to have occurred among all Athapaskans, and that these periods called for extreme measures in order to insure survival, it should be remembered that even the Eskimo, with their acknowledged specialized subsistence activities, frequently experienced similar shortages. This was a characteristic that virtually all hunting and gathering peoples shared.

Adaptation to the severe winter of the northern continental climate was itself a specialization of considerable significance. In the boreal forest, success in hunting and fishing could be achieved only by detailed, specialized knowledge of the landscape. Indians had to be thoroughly familiar with a bewildering number of hills, valleys, streams, and forests, and the extent to which they were likely to be the homes of stable concentrations of game animals. These adaptations, and others that will be discussed in subsequent chapters, show considerable sensitivity to the very definite ecological variations that characterize this vast area of inland hunting and fishing.

DWELLINGS

The dwellings of aboriginal northern Athapaskans, reflecting the extreme mobility of most of these groups, were among the simplest constructed by any people in North America. As might be expected, the simplest structures were found among the most mobile groups while more complex construction was characteristic of more sedentary peoples. In the latter case, dwelling types were sometimes less a reflection of particular cultural and environmental requirements than of borrowings from neighboring peoples. The extreme variation of the subarctic continental climate, characterized by short, hot summers and long, extremely cold winters, is a factor that must be constantly kept in mind when considering shelters in the subarctic interior. Among every Athapaskan group, the pattern of shelter reflected not only the subsistence activities characteristic of particular times of the year, but also climatic variations.

The aboriginal dwelling types of various Athapaskan groups will be described within the framework of the physiographic divisions previously described. These divisions accurately reflect the range of ecological adaptations in housing that were made throughout the area.

Although the cordilleran region has a considerable north to south range, the aboriginal dwelling types within this vast area did not exhibit a great deal of variation, and reflected the mobility that characterized the groups which inhabited the region. The Upper Tanana may be considered reasonably typical. The several types of houses utilized by these people can be grouped into two categories: semipermanent and temporary. In the former category was the circular winter house, which consisted of a frame of long, curved poles, the lower ends of which were stuck in the snow; the upper ends did not come together at the top, thus leaving a smoke hole. These poles were reinforced by being lashed to two horizontal poles, the arches of which followed the inner curve of the structure. Preferably, this framework was covered with sewn moose hides, although caribou skins could be used if the former were not available. The typical domed lodge of this type was about fourteen feet in diameter, eight feet high, and required between eighteen and twenty moose hides for its cover. Winter houses like these were confined to a number of contiguous groups in the northern cordilleran area and perhaps were best known among the Kutchin, where the form was described as early as 1847. This type of house could be moved frequently without much difficulty (see illustrations).

Summer houses among the Upper Tanana were somewhat more permanent and located near good fishing locations. These dwellings were rectangular in floor plan, with parallel series of poles driven into the ground to make an outside and an inside wall. Strips of spruce or birch bark were then laid between them. The bark sections had to be renewed frequently. Sometimes these houses were as much as twenty or thirty feet in length and were occupied by several families. Such structures among the Upper Tanana are said to have had flat roofs, but among other groups a gabled roof was probably characteristic. There were no windows and the door generally consisted of a piece of skin. A square smoke hole in the center of the roof admitted light. Along each side of the interior were low benches on which the men slept. Women slept on the floor and personal property was stored under the benches. This type of summer dwelling was widely distributed among cordilleran Athapaskans and was also used by the Atna of the Copper River basin (see illustrations).

The Upper Tanana also made a log or pole house which resembled a log cabin except that it had pairs of parallel posts at the corners and on each side of the doorway. Logs were piled between them, each log being lashed to the corner posts with willow lashing or split spruce root. The flat roof consisted of poles covered with moss or spruce bark. The entrance was through a passageway with a skin covering at each end, which served as a stormshed to keep out the cold. This type of house may not have been aboriginal, although it was present in the area as early as 1885. It was also widespread among other cordilleran tribes.

The only temporary shelters used by the Upper Tanana were of simple lean-to construction. They were covered with brush or boughs, or, if a more permanent shelter was desired, bark or moss. Often two such shelters were built facing each other with a fire between them and each side occupied by a family. This double lean-to construction is typical of many northern Athapaskans in all physiographic regions.

One other type of structure found in the cordilleran region is worth noting. This was the so-called winter moss house of the Kutchin, a more permanent type of winter dwelling than the previously described domed lodge. Such structures were built each year by two families in a good hunting territory. The winter moss house was square and the floor was excavated to a depth of a foot and a half. Posts were raised at each corner to a height of between four and six feet, and two additional posts about ten feet high stood in the middle at each end between the corners. A ridge pole joined these center posts, and parallel horizontal beams connected the corner posts. Split poles six to eight inches in diameter were then lashed vertically to this framework, a hole being left in the roof for the emission of smoke. A door was left in one end by omitting a few upright poles. The final step in construction was to pile large squares of moss and sod around the sides and end. Moss was also laid on the roof and covered with dirt. A dirt mound was built in the center of the house for a fireplace. This type of structure was occupied from about the beginning of October until early in January, when the Indians began leading a less sedentary life and moved into the dome-shaped, skin-covered structures previously described for the Upper Tanana.

Dwellings among Indians of the Arctic drainage lowlands were somewhat similar to those described above, but the skin tipi was also used in aboriginal times. Such a dwelling has been described among the Bear Lake Indians, consisting of an initial framework of several poles filled in with additional poles spaced from 18 to 36 inches apart at the base. The size of these structures varied greatly and depended upon the number of skins available for a cover. The Bear Lake tipi was open at the top and lacked the attached ring that was characteristic of the plains tipi. Caribou skins were preferred for covers, but if these were not available, moose hides were an acceptable substitute. In winter the skins were used with the hair outside, and in summer with the hair removed. The skins were dressed and then sewn with babiche or sinew. Inside, the ground was covered with spruce boughs and the fireplace in the center was protected from the brush by flat poles. In winter, snow was heaped around the edges of the skin cover to keep out the wind. It is likely, however, that these tipis were cold and drafty under the best of circumstances. The Bear Lake Indians traveled on the Barren Grounds in winter and carried their lodge poles with them. Not infrequently the number of poles would be reduced when it was necessary to use some of them for firewood.

The skin-covered tipi was used by many groups in the Mackenzie River drainage, and it has been suggested that the Dogrib, Slave, and Chipewyan may have borrowed this dwelling type from the Cree within relatively recent times. The Slave apparently did not use the tipi in summer, but instead inhabited semicircular, open shelters constructed by bending over and tying willows and then covering them with moose hides.

It is likely that even the most permanent of the structures just described was not often constructed twice in the same place. When we come to consider the dwellings of Indians in the Yukon and Kuskokwim river basins, however, we are concerned with more sedentary groups like the Ingalik who occupied permanent winter villages and summer fish camps usually not far from the winter settlements. It will be remembered that the Ingalik live in close proximity to the Eskimos of the lower Yukon. Thus their culture has been influenced in a number of ways by Eskimos and in few areas is this influence more noticeable than in housing.

The Ingalik erected at least three types of winter houses of varying sizes, all of which resembled to a marked degree the semi-subterranean, earth-covered Eskimo house of southwestern Alaska. The smaller structures were about sixteen feet long and slightly less wide. As a first step in construction, an excavation was made to a depth of approximately three and a half feet. The house roof was supported by two pairs of posts set in a parallel position against the front and back walls. Beams were stretched from front to rear between these posts. Slanting roof poles were placed all around the structure so as to extend from the ground surface about a foot and a half to two feet from the edge of the excavation to the horizontal beams. Then horizontal poles were laid across the front-to-rear beams, and the narrow central section on the roof completed by putting the final roof poles in place, leaving a smoke hole opening. The whole roof and sides were then covered with sod and grass. When no fire was burning, the smoke hole was covered. There was a roofed entryway about six feet in length at ground level and steps led to the door, which was covered with a grass mat. Inside there were benches on three sides constructed of spruce poles.

The Ingalik also made winter houses that were larger and somewhat more complex than the one just described but much the same in design. In addition, they constructed a *kashim,* or ceremonial house, which was also semi-subterranean and as much as 35 feet by 25 feet in size. It had a cribbed roof and a long entryway which widened to form a separate room. There were benches on all four sides. The *kashim,* a characteristic feature of Eskimo villages throughout southwestern Alaska, served as a sleeping room and workroom for the men, a place to take sweat baths, and a theater for religious and secular ceremonies. Both the *kashim* and the various winter houses were used during the occupation of winter villages, primarily from August until May.

A number of different types of dwellings were also constructed in summer villages or fish camps. There were above-ground, rectangular structures with pitched roofs and walls of vertically-placed spruce planks, spruce bark, or birch bark strips. The spruce plank houses were the most sturdy and were sometimes used for as many as six successive summers if the owners returned to the same summer village. The Ingalik also made smoke houses, constructed like the summer houses, for smoking fish.

In the Cook Inlet-Susitna River basin area, the Tanaina Indians, who were even more sedentary than the Ingalik, constructed a large winter house which could have several sleeping rooms and a bathhouse attached. In the Kachemak Bay area the structure was excavated to a depth of two feet and had a gabled roof. Log walls were constructed in much the same manner as the log or pole house of the Upper Tanana. All the Tanaina made semi-spherical lodges with pole frameworks and bark or grass covering for use on hunting trips during all seasons of the year. Similar structures have already been described, but those of the Tanaina had no smoke holes, the fires being built outside.

In the Copper River basin, we have much less detailed information for dwellings of the Atna than for those of tribes in the other geographical regions. It is known that the winter dwelling of these Indians was a rectangular bark house similar to that which has been described for the Upper Tanana. These houses were occupied during the period of the salmon runs and until February, at which time people moved to the headwaters of streams tributary to the Copper River. Here they constructed temporary rectangular structures of poles and spruce boughs that were essentially double lean-tos similar to those previously described. The Atna apparently had the simplest dwellings of any of the more sedentary Athapaskans.

SETTLEMENT PATTERNS

The determinants of settlement configurations throughout the area occupied by northern Athapaskans can be most profitably considered after achieving some familiarity with the patterning of the region. For this purpose it will be useful to discuss briefly the framework into which our consideration of settlement patterns will be placed.

The classification that will be employed here was originated collectively by Richard K. Beardsley and a group of colleagues for a seminar, the results of which were published in 1956. This classification is based primarily on the concept of community mobility. Communities are defined as "the largest grouping of persons in any particular culture whose normal activities bind them together into a self-conscious, corporate unit, which is economically self-sufficient and politically independent." These units become larger and more stable as food resources increase along with the people's ability to exploit them.

The authors of this typology were particularly concerned with community patterns, which are defined as the "organization of economic, socio-political, and ceremonial inter-relations within a community." Seven levels or types of community patterns are identified on a scale ranging from those groups whose members wandered freely to those communities that were permanently sedentary. In this system, community mobility is considered a function primarily of subsistence resources and technological knowledge. As more food becomes available through an increase of knowledge about exploiting the environment, populations tend to become more sedentary.

Two of Beardsley's types of community patterns are applicable to precontact northern Athapaskans. These are defined as follows:

✴ *Restricted Wandering.* Communities that wander about within a territory that they define as theirs and defend against trespass, or on which they have exclusive rights to food resources of certain kinds. Movement within the territory may be erratic or may follow a seasonal round, depending on the kind of wild food resources utilized.

✴ *Central-Based Wandering.* A community that spends part of each year wandering and the rest at a settlement or "central base," to which it may or may not consistently return in subsequent years.

What might be regarded as the "typical" northern Athapaskans, those of the northern cordilleran and northern arctic drainage lowlands regions who have been influenced only moderately by neighboring cultures, are best classified at the Restricted Wandering level. This community pattern, basic to and preparatory for later stages in the evolution of food producing, is adapted to scattered or seasonably available food resources. Population density is always low and the maximum size of the permanent community or band is small, usually less than 100 individuals. Members of a band may travel together for all or for only part of the year. The community defends its range against outsiders, but also occasionally allows other individuals or groups to exploit the territory under special conditions.

Restricted Wandering peoples exploit territory by hunting, fishing, and collecting food. Community mobility is required by the seasonal nature of the food supply or by the fact that no one area is productive enough to allow the community to remain there for long. Since Restricted Wanderers move frequently, their material culture is usually rather simple and highly portable, consisting for the most part of food-getting equipment. Virtually all edible resources of the environment are exploited, and sharing rules operate in such a manner that individual luck or skill in subsistence activities benefits everyone.

The largest social unit among Restricted Wanderers is the local group or band. It may consist of related or friendly families or a single extended family. Formal leadership is usually minimal, and if it exists at all, it is primarily of an advisory nature. Such a leader has no power to enforce his wishes. It is typical of Restricted Wanderers to have only one spouse at a time and status differences are minimal or nonexistent. Religious behavior includes a reliance on magic to bring luck in hunting and for curing.

Although Restricted Wandering is associated with those interior subarctic Athapaskans we have defined as "typical," there are some groups which occupy ecological niches that make it possible for them to be placed at the Central-Based Wandering level within the Beardsley scheme. This level is reached when it is possible for a group of people to harvest, store, and preserve a locally abundant wild food.

Because of increased food supply, the number of people sustained at the central base can reach 200 or so and they are reasonably well integrated when they are together. During part of the year, it is necessary for the people to live in self-sufficient nuclear or extended family groupings, at which time their way of life parallels that of Restricted Wanderers. Community integration is limited because of the seasonal dispersal of families from the central base and because the community may not have the same members from year to year during its sedentary phase. Thus a chief or other leader may sometimes serve as a symbol of the community, but he has no coercive power. Religious behavior characteristically involves shamans, persons having a special relationship with supernatural beings who confer the power to cure illness and bring good luck in hunting.

The annual pattern of movement for specific Athapaskan groups and subgroups is difficult to determine. Although most ethnographic monographs pay some attention to movements of people within the seasonal round, it is virtually impossible to obtain a complete statement of the settlement pattern of any specific group. Settlement patterns were one of the first aspects of

Indian culture to change after the coming of the white man. It is possible to document this change for some groups, and we will attempt to do so in a later chapter, but the purely aboriginal settlement patterns—which in some cases underwent their first changes as early as the late eighteenth century—are frequently impossible to reconstruct.

It is probably true that hunters and fishermen can operate most successfully in free-ranging units which gather together when they are able and spread out when it is necessary. A large kill from a herd of migrating caribou, for example, would often allow 100 or more individuals to stay together over a long period of time. An extensive fish run might have the same effect. Fish runs tend to be predictable and dependable in their occurrence and can mean the difference between a Restricted Wandering and a Central-Based Wandering community pattern. When game is scarce, however, people must separate into smaller groupings of perhaps only three or four nuclear families which spread out over a wide area. Of course, small groupings like this were in touch with one another and thus ready to help each other in times of difficulty. People felt free to move back and forth between groupings and to hunt outside their usual areas when game was scarce.

There can be little doubt that in aboriginal times the greatest number of Athapaskans were Restricted Wanderers, and that only those people situated along the major rivers of western Alaska or the sea coast of Cook Inlet enjoyed an environment sufficiently rich in wild food resources to permit the more settled way of life associated with the Central-Based Wandering community pattern. Thus most of the groups in the cordilleran area and the Arctic drainage lowlands that depended heavily on the hunting of large game animals were Restricted Wanderers. Fishing was also important to these people and, indeed, frequently sustained them in times of game shortage, but it did not play the major role in their subsistence cycle that it did for those Indians living along the Yukon River and its tributaries.

Perhaps a typical example of Restricted Wanderers in the arctic drainage lowlands were the Peel River Kutchin, inhabitants of the drainage of that river, a tributary of the Mackenzie, which flows in a generally southward direction out of the Ogilvie Mountains. In the protocontact period, which for this area is the late eighteenth and early nineteenth century, the Peel River people spent their winters in the mountains on both sides of the Mackenzie-Yukon divide. The location of the population and whether it was concentrated or dispersed depended on the availability of game, particularly caribou. This animal was very important to the people both for their own use and for trade with other groups. Although the situation might change from year to year, people generally were dispersed during the late fall until herds of caribou were located. If the animals were found in sufficient numbers, several large units were then formed to hunt them by means of surrounds, a method that has already been described. Most of the cooperative hunting took place during the early winter. In the late eighteenth and early nineteenth centuries, the Peel River Kutchin were also involved to some extent in fur trapping, and this individually-oriented activity took up much of the later part of the winter.

Before the Peel River ice broke up in the late spring, the Indians moved down the upper Peel and its tributaries toward one or more gathering places on the lower river. Travel was very slow at this time of the year as people had to proceed on foot or on toboggans pulled by other people. Although some families might own one or two dogs which were used for hunting, dog team travel was not introduced until the fur trade was well developed in the nineteenth century.

By the time the ice had broken up and the river was clear and high, the Peel River Kutchin were gathered at three or four fishing camps along the lower river. This was a time of year when games and ceremonies were held and when raiding and warfare with the neighboring Mackenzie Eskimos took place. In summer, following a season of fishing and leisurely life, the larger groups in the fish camps would break up and return once more to the mountainous areas of the upper river.

The typical Central-Based Wandering pattern was found among those Athapaskans who occupy the Yukon and Kuskokwim river basins and the Cook Inlet-Susitna River basin. In this area, as we have seen, the availability of predictable runs of salmon each summer gave a measure of stability to the way of life that was lacking among the Athapaskans in the Mackenzie drainage region. The Ingalik of the lower Yukon, for example, occupied winter villages from August to May and then moved to their summer fish camps. Summer villages or camps were usually close to good fishing places, and often not far from the winter villages. Sometimes the fish camps were directly in front of the winter villages, always close to the bank, or perhaps right across the river. The summer villages, whether adjacent to the winter villages or separate from them, were always smaller than the winter communities because the people spread out to take advantage of the best fishing sites in the area. Some villages were occupied in both winter and summer, from which people departed in late spring for temporary residence in fish camps.

The Ingalik relied heavily on summer fishing and their absences from the winter villages for hunting were generally of short duration unless elaborate, cooperative caribou hunting was involved. For these specialized fishermen, winter could be a time of relative leisure when elaborate ceremonies were held in the *kashim*. The way of life of the Ingalik, Koyukon, Tanana, and Tanaina resembled to a marked degree that of riverine Eskimos throughout southwestern Alaska.

Chapter 3

SOCIAL INSTITUTIONS

In discussing northern Athapaskan social institutions, a greater degree of generalization is possible than in our treatment of subsistence activities. From what has been said about Restricted Wanderers and Central-Based Wanderers, it should be apparent that differences between them with reference to social organization were more a matter of degree than of kind. Nevertheless, it will be necessary to devote some attention to those circumstances under which the social relations of certain Athapaskan groups have been influenced, and even to some extent determined, by their proximity to other cultures. The general diffusiveness of Athapaskan social organization has made many groups particularly susceptible to such outside influences.

We have already noted the absence of any concept of group identification beyond that of territory or language, but each of the identified groups is divided into subgroups, and it is these subgroups rather than the larger enclaves that have social meaning to the people themselves. While such names as Ingalik, Kutchin, Dogrib, or Slave had no social reality to the people involved, the subdivisions had not only territorial and possibly linguistic significance, but their membership included people who had frequent face-to-face contact with one another, who traveled and lived together, and who shared reciprocal obligations toward one another.

A serious difficulty which impedes our attempts to understand aboriginal northern Athapaskan social organization is the many changes brought about by contact with Europeans and the subsequent development of the fur trade. In some areas, these changes began in the eighteenth century, and it is frequently impossible at this distance in time to trace them to their foreign source. Thus, an aspect of social organization that may appear at first glance to have been a part of aboriginal Athapaskan culture may, in fact, be the result of changes introduced early in the contact period.

BAND ORGANIZATION

Evidence indicates that during the aboriginal period, resources within the territories of the various Athapaskan groups were available to all who needed them. When there was no game in a particular area, the people who had been hunting there felt perfectly free to move into an area being exploited by neighbors, and there appears to have been no resentment on the part of those who shared their resources. It should be emphasized, however, that this kind of sharing among subgroups was usually confined within the larger boundaries of a single group. Even these boundaries were doubtless flexible; the reader will recall our earlier reference to the Ingalik of the lower Innoko River who frequently hunted caribou in the territory of the neighboring Koyukon.

We have spoken here of "groups" and "subgroups" and we now must consider the nature of the ties within and between such units. Most aboriginal northern Athapaskans spent at least part of the year in small aggregates consisting of a few nuclear families. Various authors have suggested names for these aggregates, the most meaningful of which include hunting group, task group, local band, and microcosmic group.

At certain times of the year, the ecology of an area permitted several small units of the type just mentioned to come together to form what has been called a band. Other names for this combined grouping are regional band or macrocosmic group. Summer fishing and fall caribou migrations are good examples of the kinds of situations that permitted local bands to gather as a regional band. The whole band was usually associated with a particular region, shaped in large measure by the drainage pattern of the land, since summer canoe routes and winter dog-team trails followed lakes or rivers and their tributaries. Thus the Ingalik were divided into four subgroups, or regional bands, each of which was associated with a particular part of the total territory. The size of these subgroup territories and the nature of Ingalik subsistence was such that there was little face-to-face contact between many members of the band, even when some degree of kin relationship might exist between them. The Slave are described as having been divided into four or five dialect subgroups, each with a membership of approximately 200 individuals. It is not clear, however, that linguistic differences were always a feature of band organization among the various Athapaskan groups.

Observation of band organization today suggests that in aboriginal times relations between the smaller local hunting bands within the regional band involved many ties of both blood and marriage. Therefore, it should be remembered that when these local bands gathered together they were meeting with their kinsmen and not simply with neighbors. This made it possible for some families to shift their affiliation from one small hunting aggregate to another when the regional band broke up at the end of a fishing period or caribou migration.

Considerable research has been done recently by June Helm on the social groupings of the Dogrib Indians, which may be considered reasonably typical of Mackenzie drainage people. Three kinds of socio-territorial groups have been identified among the Dogrib: the regional band, the local band, and the task group. Membership in these units was not mutually exclusive; a person could, and usually did, have a social identity in all three. There were, however, certain features that characterized each socio-territorial unit.

The regional band exploited the total range of the band as identified by tradition and use. It utilized all the resources within the range, and this total territory provided sufficient food and other resources to sustain life except during periodic famines. Therefore, the regional band could exist for many generations. At the turn of the century, by no means the aboriginal period for the Dogrib, there were four or five regional bands. It is characteristic of the regional band, as we have noted, to be physically dispersed much of the time. The families who belonged to it were likely to come together when operating as a task group exploiting a resource which, by its nature, allowed a large number of persons to congregate, such as a fall fishing camp. Most of the time, the various families making up the regional band were dispersed in smaller units. Regional band members, however, were related through a network of primary affinal and consanguinal ties.

The local band also exploited its smaller range, which was usually a segment of the regional band territory, and like the regional band, it exploited all the resources within its territory. It was essentially a grouping of close kinsmen and tended to have greater spatial cohesion than the regional band. Its temporal duration was related to the activities for which it was organized and changing membership meant that any particular local band might be in existence only a generation or two. It was, of course, much smaller than the regional band; whereas the latter might have as many as 100 married couples plus their dependents, the local band was likely to average four couples together with their offspring and other dependents. Members of a local band might consist of a core of siblings, male and female, with their spouses and dependents.

The task group was generally a grouping for the express purpose of exploiting a specific seasonal resource. By definition the task group did not survive beyond the period required to perform the task for which it was constituted. Its membership might include a conjugal pair or two with dependents, or it might be all male. Kinship ties were often significant in forming task groups, but such factors as friendship and special abilities were also important. Task groups varied in size depending on the purpose for which they were formed. Two or three nuclear families, frequently linked by sibling or parent-child relationship, might join together for periods of several weeks or months for trapping along with general subsistence activities.

The difference between a task group and a local band was one of degree rather than kind. At certain seasons of the year, a task group could be quite sizeable, particularly if it were formed to exploit good fishing or to take advantage of a caribou migration. At these times, the task group would approximate the size of a local band, or even of the regional band itself, differing from these groupings only in terms of temporal duration. In other words, in some areas, and under certain circumstances, both the local and the regional band could function as task groups.

The band concept as just described can also be applied to the more settled northern Athapaskans, those who have previously been defined as Central-Based Wanderers. Among these people, most of whom are to be found in the western Athapaskan area in Alaska, the central base or village played an important part in social organization and as a center for exploiting the resources of the environment. The Ingalik, for example, were divided into four subgroups as follows: (1) the Anvik-Shageluk group centering around the villages of the same names; (2) the Bonasila group in the vicinity of that village; (3) the Holy Cross-Georgetown group in the neighborhood of those communities; and (4) the McGrath group, which included the people of the drainage of the upper Kuskokwim River. These groupings might be considered roughly equivalent to regional bands, while the specific communities within the subgroups approximate local bands. The flexibility of membership that characterized the regional and local bands of the Mackenzie drainage Athapaskans was also characteristic of Ingalik subgroups and villages. The task group was also characteristic of Central-Based Wanderers, and the Ingalik in particular frequently formed such units for hunting and trapping, as well as at summer fishing camps. It is clear, therefore, that in matters of organization, at least on the broad levels related to ecological adaptation, the difference between Central-Based Wanderers and Restricted Wanderers was not great.

Unfortunately for our understanding of precontact band organization, after the beginning of the historic period several bands occasionally gathered at a single point to trade. It is regrettable that in the literature these aggregations are also called bands, making it almost impossible to determine with accuracy the largest group which people named and with which they identified. Trading posts heavily influenced all territorial alignments and effectively obliterated the precontact groupings. In recent times, some of the trading post aggregates have been large, the Dogrib band in the vicinity of Fort Rae, for example, numbering in excess of 1200 persons.

LEADERSHIP AND WARFARE

Within northern Athapaskan regional and local bands, there was little role differentiation involved in the decision-making process; all the adult males attempted to achieve a consensus when policies were to be made. Nevertheless, regional bands as well as smaller groupings often had leaders who attained prestige and influence through a demonstration of their superior abilities, particularly as hunters. Such leadership rested entirely on the force of an individual's personality and his ability to demonstrate his skill at locating and killing game animals. Once he ceased to exhibit these qualities, his claims to leadership and influence quickly disappeared.

leadership qualities

Local bands and task groups were frequently organized around such leaders. A number of families would place themselves under the leadership of a skilled hunter and his suggestions would be followed as to the direction of movement or the subsistence activity that could best be practiced at a particular time and in a particular location. Since such leadership rested entirely on a realistic appraisal of the leader's skills and his value as a provider to the group, membership in any particular aggregate might change radically when a given leader ceased to manifest the necessary qualities of leadership. Thus the precise composition of a task group might depend just as much on the leader as it did on the task being performed.

Among certain groups such as the Dogrib and Chipewyan in which communal hunting on a large scale frequently took place, leadership assumed greater importance than among others such as the Slave, where subsistence activities tended to be more individualized. A communal caribou hunt involving the construction of a corral and the organization of large numbers of people to drive the animals toward their eventual ensnarement obviously required leadership of a higher order than that necessary when two or three hunters were pursuing a moose in wooded country (see illustrations). A leader of the former activity would also receive much greater recognition, at least for the duration of the caribou drive.

Both offensive and defensive warfare were known among northern Athapaskans and this type of activity frequently led to another kind of leader: the war leader. These individuals were usually aggressive men who dominated through their physical strength. The Chandalar Kutchin, for example, had two types of leader: the successful hunter and trapper who was consequently a wealthy man, and the war leader. Before European contact, individuals occupying the latter role were said to have been very powerful and, on occasion, to have killed people who did not obey their orders. Apparently this kind of leader could maintain at least some aspects of his authority even during times of peace. Hereditary leadership occurred only rarely; however, a son might succeed his father if he happened to possess the right personal qualifications. This probably happened often, since a son was brought up to emulate the skills and abilities of his father. In any event, it is clear that among all northern Athapaskans, the role of leader was based on personal qualities and not associated with political activity in any way.

Wealth played a larger role in leadership in some groups than in others. Among the Upper Tanana, for example, leadership could not be attained solely by the accumulation of wealth, but such wealth did enable an individual to give frequent potlatches and thereby earn a reputation as a lavish spender. The mechanics of the potlatch will be considered later in this chapter. Here it is sufficient to point out that it was a gift-giving festival in honor of a dead relative; unlike the comparable institution on the northwest coast, the gifts gathered no interest and were not returned. Through the potlatch, an individual expressed his desire for prestige. Even among tribes such as the Upper Tanana, who practiced the potlatch and emphasized it as the basis of all social position, it was still the good hunter or the successful trapper who became an acknowledged leader. Thus the ecological imperatives of subsistence took precedence over an elaboration of the social organization.

Hereditary leaders did occur among some northern Athapaskans, particularly in the extreme western groups such as the Tahltan, Carrier, Chilcotin, and perhaps the Tanana. Among these groups, leadership tended to be linked with the system of matrilineal sibs about which more will be said presently. In other groups, however, the basic idea of the Athapaskan leader as an individual possessed of important subsistence skills, but having only very limited power, was combined with an insistence, as among the Upper Tanana, that the leader be liberal with his gifts.

Turning again to warfare, we find that it was more widespread than might have been expected for a people whose major efforts were presumably directed toward subsistence. Generally speaking, war represented retaliation for offenses committed by relative strangers upon members of the group. Since revenge in turn promoted the desire for fresh vengence on the part of the opposite side, antagonism between groups could be chronic. This type of hostile behavior more closely resembles feuding than it does the conventional notion of warfare. Ingalik fights with their upper Yukon Athapaskan neighbors usually originated in some insignificant difficulty, and tension might build up over a number of years before an actual attack was carried out. War, therefore, was defensive, at least in theory—a means of subduing bad or potentially dangerous people.

Among most Athapaskans, war involved surprise attacks at night, slaughtering or carrying off women and children, capture of booty, and forays of greatly superior forces against an enemy previously determined to be weak. However, hand-to-hand encounters using knives, spears, and clubs were not unknown. Peel River Kutchin fighting men set off in large groups together, hoping to come upon the enemy unawares, catching them in their houses. The entryways were then blocked and the houses set on fire by pouring oil over them.

Warfare between Athapaskans and their non-Athapaskan-speaking neighbors was common. The Chandalar Kutchin and Tanaina frequently fought with the Eskimo, while the Eskimo and Cree both fought the Chipewyan. Groups which waged war with the Eskimo apparently did so primarily to capture their possessions, which had trophy value and served to enhance the prestige of the owner.

Wars involving the Cree and Chipewyan played a major part in the movement of peoples within the western interior. In fact, intergroup warfare increased considerably after European contact and largely centered on securing favorable positions with reference to the fur trade. Success or failure in these postcontact wars was directly related to success in obtaining firearms. The Cree obtained firearms before most Athapaskans did and, in addition to fighting the Chipewyan, frequently attacked the Sekani and carried off women to become their wives. The Sekani and other southern cordilleran peoples apparently had a more exclusive concept of territoriality than most other Athapaskans and frequently killed intruders. This may have been due to the closer proximity of linguistically and culturally unrelated peoples in this area.

A variety of weapons appear to have been used by the Athapaskans for warlike purposes, including knives, spears, and bows and arrows. The Upper Tanana had a specialized adze constructed expressly for war purposes that must have inflicted grievous wounds. On the march these weapons were carried with the handle stuck down the back of the shirt so that they could not be seen as the enemy was approached. Slat armor similar to that found among the Eskimo and along the Pacific Coast was used, most prominently by the western Athapaskan groups in Alaska.

SOCIAL RELATIONS

The basic unit of social organization among northern Athapaskans, as among all peoples, was the nuclear family consisting of a man, his wife or wives, and their natural or adopted children. Throughout much of the Athapaskan area, extended kinship was characterized by the presence of matrilineal sib organization, consanguinal kin groups which acknowledged a traditional bond of common descent in the maternal line, but were not always able to trace the actual geneological connection between individuals. These sibs, which were tied together in a network of reciprocal obligations, generally were exogamous; that is, a person had to find a mate outside his sib. In more recent times, however, there is evidence that the rules of exogamy have been less rigorously enforced. Sib affiliations also played an important part in warfare, marriages, funerals, and potlatches. They were frequently not localized but were spread over large areas, even though they might have had different names in bands that were widely separated.

The number of sibs tended to vary among different groups, but there were usually three, one of these being vaguely defined. When two sibs recognize a more tenuous bond of kinship than that which characterizes each of them independently, the grouping is known as a phratry. If only two sibs are functional, every person is necessarily a member of one or the other and the term moiety is applied to the pair. Phratry and moiety organization, like sib affiliation, could affect various aspects of the individual's social life. The sib system is no longer fully operative in any Athapaskan group and has not been for some time. Thus there is some confusion among anthropologists, and even in the minds of the Indians themselves, concerning their function. In any event, it is no longer possible to obtain a satisfactory explanation of the tripartite system.

Athapaskan specialists have directed considerable attention to the question of whether or not matrilineal sib organization spread inland from the coast during protohistoric or early historic times. This inland spread may have occurred because the availability of new goods, particularly European trade materials, encouraged intensive trade between Athapaskans and their coastal neighbors. It is known, for example, that the coastal Tlingit had a complex matrilineal organization in the protohistoric period, characterized by an elaborate art and special songs and dances. By early historic times, and perhaps even earlier, the Tutchone and Tagish had Tlingit-like sibs, some known by Tlingit names in the Athapaskan dialects. This Tlingit social organization apparently spread as a result of intermarriage, but most recent research suggests that it was superimposed on an already existing system of matrilineal reckoning.

Matrilineal sibs were found among the Atna on the Copper River, in the Tanana and Yukon drainages, among the Tanaina, the Tanana, and the Kutchin, although they apparently faded out among the eastern Kutchin. Further to the east the Kaska had coastal-influenced matrilineal sibs, as did the Tahltan and the Carrier. Among other eastern Athapaskans, however, both the maternal and paternal lines were relevant for purposes of tracing descent and this bilateral (as opposed to unilateral) reckoning was also characteristic of two groups in western Alaska, the Ingalik and Koyukon.

Students of social organization have generally attributed the unilineality of many Athapaskans either to a riverine existence and dependence on salmon, a subsistence activity in which women have a major role, or to diffusion from the northwest coast. Athapaskan specialists no longer believe that most groups were as dependent on fish as had been previously supposed, but they are inclined to feel that the diffusion explanation is too simplistic. Thus they are now generally of the opinion that matriliny in the area is a very old practice. Some have suggested that the ancestors of the Na-Dene peoples brought the remnants of Old World matrilineal organization with them and that these were subsequently lost by the bilateral eastern groups. Others believe that a bilateral form of social organization has greater survival value in the subarctic because it makes possible a larger number and variety of kinship affiliations in a difficult environment where assistance from kinsmen is essential for survival. It certainly appears true that the sparse population of the area, a reflection, at least in part, of the demanding ecological situation, caused the sib system among northern Athapaskans to function under considerable stress. Migrations, emigrations, and the ravages of war and disease were doubtless also significant factors. These circumstances would explain some of the confusion that exists about the system among both Indians and ethnologists at the present time. Since the origin of matriliny has some bearing on theoretical considerations related to early hunting and gathering societies, we will return to this question toward the end of the chapter.

Among small hunting and gathering aggregates like Athapaskan bands, emphasis was on immediate kinship concerns, and there were few mechanisms by which the responsibilities of kinship could be extended to non-kin. One such mechanism was wife sharing, which is mentioned for a number of groups without the implications being entirely clear. The custom does not seem to have had the same responsibilities associated with it as, for example, among the Eskimos. Polygyny, the marriage of one man to two or more wives at a time, occurred occasionally, the wives usually being sisters. Polyandry, the union of one woman with two or more men at one time was also practiced, but much more rarely. Neither of these customs could be widespread among people living close to the basic subsistence level. The levirate, whereby a widow marries her deceased husband's brother, was also characteristic of many northern Athapaskan groups, but the sororate, which sanctions the marriage of a widower with the sister of his deceased wife, was rare. Both customs are designed to insure the continuance of the nuclear family with its responsibilities and obligations after the death of a spouse.

Matrilocal residence, whereby a newly married couple lives with or near the bride's family, was characteristic throughout much of the area. Frequently, as among the Tanana and Kutchin, it followed a year or more of bride service during which the husband worked for his new father-in-law. After the marriage, the couple lived in the dwelling of the wife's parents, but following the birth of the first child, the growing family usually established a separate residence in the local or regional band where they had previously lived. Among those Athapaskan groups where bilaterality was characteristic, it is possible that residence patterns were more flexible and individual choice played a greater role.

At the present time, a married couple may live with a group containing members of the husband's family (virilocal) or the wife's (uxorilocal). It is rare, however, for them to live apart from both. Recent investigators note that their Athapaskan informants usually have little to say concerning residence rules. Since nuclear families frequently transfer their residence from one local or regional band to another, it follows that residence after marriage is more likely to be determined by demographic and ecological factors than by hard and fast rules. As June Helm (Helm and Leacock, 1971) has noted, such rules are apt to be more important to anthropologists than they are to the Indians.

The question of band exogamy is also relevant, but an intelligent discussion of the subject is dependent on our ability to distinguish the characteristics of a band. As we have seen, this is not easy. Obviously, the small hunting group of closely related families could not offer a potential spouse to everyone contemplating marriage, but the larger, although frequently dispersed, regional band might easily provide one. Thus it can be said that the larger the group under consideration, the more endogamous (within-the-group) marriages were likely to occur. In any event, proximity was certainly a major factor in determining marriage partners among Athapaskans as in our own society, and a man did not go far afield to look for a wife.

In conclusion, residence alternatives, shifting local and regional band membership, and a wide choice of marriage partners tended to create multiple affiliations for an individual, which extended from his local band to a much wider area. Thus the number of persons in different places on whom he could count for assistance in time of need was considerable, an important consideration under ecological conditions where the threat of starvation was very real.

THE POTLATCH

An important feature of social organization among many Athapaskans was the potlatch, a ceremony in honor of the dead that is best known as it occurred among the Indians of the northwest coast. Among Athapaskans, the potlatch existed in one form or another in all the western tribes but was not found among any of those in the Mackenzie drainage. This fact has led to the general belief that the trait diffused from the northwest coast into the Athapaskan area.

Among the Upper Tanana, even today the potlatch permeates virtually every phase of the social life of the people. On the surface, it is simply a feast for the dead. Indians explain that a family is overwhelmed by sorrow after a death and that its headman, in order to forget his grief, holds a potlatch at which there is much feasting, dancing, and general merrymaking, climaxed by a distribution of gifts. At the conclusion of the festivities, the leader is spiritually rejuvenated and the deceased is socially forgotten.

This explanation of the potlatch, although it probably accounts for the ceremony's origin, does not provide a true picture of its importance as a social institution. In actuality, the potlatch was the chief means by which an individual achieved prestige in his own and neighboring bands. If a man aspired to be a leader, he had to give a potlatch whenever possible and the death of even a distant relative provided an excuse to celebrate. It was necessary for him to have a sufficient store of food and blankets to give away on these occasions.

The potlatch was not only an important social and ceremonial occasion for the man who was giving it, but was also one of the few occasions when the Upper Tanana gathered together as a group. This ceremonial function helps to explain why the potlatch has continued to be important down to the present time, in spite of the objections of missionaries—who believed it to be a heathen custom—and of traders, who objected to the diversion of energies from trapping.

Several years might elapse between a man's death and the potlatch honoring him. The person giving the ceremony would use the time to accumulate stores for the event. These would include not only blankets, rifles, calico, and other items, but also food, since the entire gathering had to be fed. Articles intended for a potlatch were sacred once they had been gathered for that purpose and families were known to starve rather than eat any of the food that had been set aside in anticipation. When everything was ready, the host sent a messenger to neighboring bands to invite them to the ceremony. When the guests arrived, they were welcomed with feasting, singing, and dancing, and this would continue as long as the host was able to provide food. On the final day of the festival, the guests put on a dinner that was considered payment for their entertainment. After that, gifts were distributed, not equally, but with the older and more important men receiving the greatest share.

The man who gave the potlatch had to give away all the property he owned and could not accept aid from anyone for a year following the ceremony. There were also a number of taboos to which he was supposed to adhere for varying periods of time. These were similar to the taboos associated with critical periods in the life cycle of the individual, thus emphasizing the fact that, having given a potlatch, a man was supposed to be spiritually renewed. The penalty for avoiding or breaking any of the taboos associated with the post-potlatch period was poor luck in hunting. This in turn would of course influence a man's ability to give future potlatches.

The Upper Tanana potlatch was similar to that of the Tahltan, Carrier, Han, Atna, and Tlingit, in that it was on the surface a feast of the dead but in reality a means of achieving prestige. Less formalized potlatches were also given by the Tanana, Koyukon, Ingalik, and Kutchin.

A considerable amount of attention has been paid to resemblances between Athapaskan potlatches and those of the northwest coast, particularly of the Tlingit. Some authorities are of the opinion that the potlatch was borrowed directly from these more elaborate societies, and there is no denying the obvious Tlingit influences on the ceremony as it is performed by the Upper Tanana. However, recent students of Athapaskan culture have discovered that some of these shared elements are common to much of the interior regions and to all the western Athapaskan groups. Therefore, it is possible that many of the cultural elements common to the western Athapaskans and the Tlingit may be traits that were part of an earlier cultural level shared by the people of both areas. Nevertheless, the western Athapaskans transformed the potlatch from the community rite that it was among the Tlingit and other northwest coast groups to an essentially individualistic one. This may be related to the limited availability of surplus food, even in the western Athapaskan area where the environment permits a Central-Based Wandering settlement pattern. These limitations may also account for the absence of the potlatch in the Mackenzie drainage.

CONCLUSION

Band organization among northern Athapaskans has been of interest to those anthropologists particularly concerned with social organization theory. More than fifteen years ago Julian Steward identified the socio-territorial organization of the northeastern Athapaskans as the "composite hunting band" type. By this he meant that the bands consisted of unrelated nuclear families with bilateral descent and no fixed rules of residence. He correlated this type of band with cooperative hunting of large herds of game animals. More recently, Elman Service reevaluated Steward's ideas from an evolutionary perspective and suggested that "composite" bands were a post-European contact phenomenon, at least among most of the eastern Athapaskans. He assumed that the aboriginal hunting band was patrilocal with reciprocal band exogamy resulting in cross-cousin marriage; that is, a man must marry the daughter of his father's sister or his mother's brother. According to this theory, the composite band was purely a development of the historic period and resulted from catastrophic epidemics introduced after European contact.

Evidence obtained by the most recent research, although containing many gaps, indicates that in most cases the bands were indeed composite in that they contained two or more families, but that these families were likely to be related by both sib and affinal ties, were for the most part unilineal, and had at least suggested rules of residence. It is certainly true that epidemics in the early contact period created depopulation and dislocations of varying degrees of severity, but the data available suggest that considerable flexibility in social organization always existed.

It is necessary to note, therefore, that the supposition that matriliny is old runs counter to the theories of Steward and Service. In their discussion of Athapaskans, both authors make exceptions for the matrilineal Athapaskans of the western areas and stress the importance of salmon fishing in this connection. This appears to be an over-simplification of both the ecological and cultural situation, for caribou hunting was in some cases of equal or greater importance to western groups of the Pacific drainage. Both authors place greater emphasis on the possibility that matrilineality diffused from the coast than we have given here. In any event, it is clear that initial matrilocal residence was the rule among most northern Athapaskans whether or not the reckoning of kin was matrilineal or bilateral. In the last analysis, the fact remains that European contact throughout the area is comparatively recent, whereas the bands have long been composite with matrilineal descent in some cases and matrilocal residence.

Finally, we might note that Athapaskan unilinear descent groups actually do perform corporate functions and are not simply identification units. They are relevant to marriage and also play a role in life cycle observances, particularly at the time of death. These are minimal corporate functions, however, and it is clear that these descent groups are structurally less significant than similar groups in societies in many other parts of the world.

Kutchin dance, 1840 s (from Richardson, 1851, vol.1, opp. p. 397).

The Hudson Bay Company post at Fort Yukon, 1868 (from Whymper, 1869, p. 250).

Kutchin hunters, 1840s (from J. Richardson, *Arctic Searching Expedition*, London, Longman, Brown, Green and Longmans, 1851, vol. 1, opp. p. 377).

Indians hunting moose near Nulato, 1868 (from F. Whymper, *Travel and Adventure in the Territory of Alaska*, New York, Harper and Brothers, 1869, p. 244).

A Yukon River trading post about 1900 (from J. C. Cantwell, *Report of the Operations of the U.S. Revenue Steamer "Nunivak"...* Washington, D.C., Government Printing Office, 1902, opp. p. 140).

An Atna family and dwelling about 1900 (from W. R. Abercrombie, *Copper River Exploring Expedition*, Washington, D.C., Government Printing Office, 1900, pl. 158).

A Chipewyan Indian checking his net set under the ice, 1960 (photographed by the author, from VanStone, 1963, fig. 3).

A Kutchin winter scene, 1840s (from J. Richardson, *Arctic Searching Expedition,* London, Longman, 1851, Frontispiece).

Making a fish trap at Anvik, an Ingalik village on the Yukon
River, about 1925 (courtesy of National Anthropological
Archives, Smithsonian Institution).

Drying fish at an Ingalik camp near Anvik (courtesy of National Anthropological Archives, Smithsonian Institution).

An Ingalik Indian removing fish from a trap set under the ice, 1898 (courtesy of National Anthropological Archives, Smithsonian Institution).

An Ingalik fish camp on the Yukon near Anvik, about 1920 (courtesy of National Anthropological Archives, Smithsonian Institution).

Caches in an Ingalik community near Anvik, 1917 (courtesy of National Anthropological Archives, Smithsonian Institution).

A Chipewyan Indian cleaning a porcupine, 1960 (photograph by the author).

Chipewyan women preparing a moose hide (photograph by the author).

Sekani women gathering wood, about 1900 (from R.P.A.-G.
Morice, *Essai l'Origine des Denes de l'Amerique du Nord,
Quebec,* 1916, opp. p. 98).

Tanana Indian leaders about 1905 (from H. Struck, *Ten Thousand Miles with a Dog Sled*, New York, Scribner's, 1917, opp. p. 257).

A Chipewyan dog team and driver, 1960 (photograph by the author).

Koyukon Indians checking their fish traps—1868 (from F. Whymper, *Voyages et Aventures dans la Colombie Anglaise, L'Ile Vancouver, le Territoire d'Alaska et la California*, Paris, Librairie Hachette, 1880, p. 101).

A Tanana fish camp—about 1907 (courtesy of the Alaska State Library).

A Tanana mother and children—about 1907 (courtesy of the Alaska State Library).

A Tanana Indian—about 1907 (courtesy of the Alaska State Library).

Chapter 4

RELIGION AND THE SUPERNATURAL

If one were to select the single most consistent feature of aboriginal northern Athapaskan magico-religious belief systems, it would be the significant reciprocal relationship that existed between men and the animals on which they were dependent for their livelihood. Superior-subordinate aspects were largely absent from this relationship, possibly because of a widespread belief in reincarnation in animal form. This belief tended to blur the distinction between animals and men, and to emphasize the fact that the spirits of animals had to be placated if men were to continue their exploitative relationship to the natural environment.

Another characteristic feature of traditional northern Athapaskan religion was its individualism. The cultures of hunting peoples must of necessity socialize individuals to a high degree of independence, since survival depends to a large degree on individual skills. From the standpoint of religion, this meant that a great deal of emphasis was placed on individual rituals rather than on community rites. We have noted that Athapaskans did not form strong social ties beyond the immediate family, and as a result, the kinds of group ceremonies that are designed to reinforce extended kinship ties were not in most cases a significant aspect of the religion. Just as the socialization process reinforced independence at the expense of wider kinship and community ties, so the religious belief system reinforced a strong sense of generalized morality as distinct from group loyalty.

Several authorities on northern Athapaskan religion have cited as an aspect of individualism, the considerable variation in beliefs that was characteristic of different persons sharing the same religious heritage. Each individual tended to select from the belief systems of the culture those concepts that seemed particularly suitable to his own needs. Since so many beliefs were associated with game animals and with hunting, it is to be expected that the beliefs and practices of a skilled hunter were likely to be accepted by a good many others. In any event, the highly individualized character of religion meant that each person had leeway in developing his own specific attitudes and ideas about the supernatural, within the general framework of Athapaskan beliefs. Under these circumstances, it is predictable that conflicts and inconsistencies occurred and that any description of the belief system of a particular group could not be considered entirely characteristic of any one individual within that group.

ORIGIN OF THE WORLD AND MAN

The mythology of northern Athapaskans is quite complex and this has frequently been attributed to the fact that much of it was derived from adjacent areas. Figures such as Raven and various other tricksters, some in human form, which are known to Alaskan Eskimos and the northwest coast peoples, also occur in the mythology of the Athapaskan groups.

Although most Athapaskans do not appear to have been greatly concerned with cosmological questions and their speculation about such matters is unelaborated, their myths provide answers to most of the great mysteries with which men everywhere are concerned. The Chandalar Kutchin, for example, have a cycle of myths which tells how Raven created the world and the celestial bodies. One of these myths maintains that all the people in the world once lived on a single small island. Occasionally a bit of land would appear on the horizon and the people would attempt to hit it with their spears, knowing that if they could hit this bit of land, much more would appear. One day Raven came along in his canoe, hit the piece of land with his spear, and immediately a great expanse of dry land appeared. Another myth in the same cycle describes how Raven stole the moon from Bear, who kept it in a bag which hung by his bed. Both stories show Raven in the role of trickster as well as creator. In the first he steals the people's belongings when they go to capture the sea mammals stranded on the new dry land, and in the second he puts Bear to sleep by telling stories so that Fox can make off with the bag containing the moon.

Athapaskan mythology also deals with animals in the environment and explains how they came to have their present characteristics. In an Upper Tanana myth, Beaver is described as having a small tail and Muskrat a large one. Because of a discrepancy in the sizes of animals and tails, a trade is arranged so that Beaver and Muskrat come to possess their present tails.

A survey of Athapaskan myths clearly indicates that there was widespread belief in a mythological period during which the world and specific natural environments were in the process of creation. Both men and animals played major roles in this process and possessed essentially the same characteristics.

The Athapaskans were fond of storytelling, and there is a good deal more to their myths than the cosmological content just discussed. In fact, the myths can be relied upon to give valuable insights into many different aspects of the aboriginal way of life. Naturally enough, the extreme importance of the food quest, techniques for taking game, and the importance of sharing food resources figure prominently in the mythology of all Athapaskan groups. Beliefs and attitudes, war practices, the complexities of interpersonal relations, and, of course, shamanism, are also illuminated in the stories.

Perhaps the commonest type of story can hardly be described as a myth at all, being little more than an exaggerated narration of actual historical events. Such stories often account for movements of people and other events in inter- and intra-group relations. It is almost certain that the myths and stories of all groups gained a great deal in the telling. Since sex and bodily functions were treated casually, many of the stories are quite earthy, and the Indians found them highly amusing.

Although the heros in the myths that have cosmological significance always possess some degree of magical power, in no case do we find that these mythological figures were considered to be deities, nor were there any rites or ceremonies connected with the memory of their deeds. It is true that some Athapaskans seemed to describe their culture hero as having the attributes of a supreme being, but they probably did not regard him in a way that can be equated with the God of the Hebraic-Christian tradition. Today among the Kaska, for example, creation is attributed to God who is called *tenatiia,* a term designating a rich and powerful person. The present-day Indians imply that *tenatiia* has always existed, but not as a supreme deity. In their traditional creation myths, a major, active role was taken by the culture hero Crow, but nobody regards Crow and God as identical.

There are extensive published collections of Athapaskan myths and stories, since they were relatively easy material for investigators to collect. If the stories appear to be uneven in richness of detail, this should not be attributed to any inherent feature of the mythology of a particular group, but rather as a reflection of the varying skill of informants and interpreters as well as their degree of familiarity with the English language.

SPIRITS, SUPERNATURAL BEINGS, AND MAGICO-RELIGIOUS BELIEFS AND PRACTICES

Aboriginal northern Athapaskans lived in a world of multitudinous spirits which influenced every aspect of their lives and destinies. These spirits were found everywhere and in relation to everything. There were impersonal spirits which animated the elements of nature, such as fire, the wind, and rivers. There was the human spirit or soul which on a person's death went to live in the land of the dead. And, of course, there were the spirits of animals, which were certainly the most numerous and perhaps the most important of all. Athapaskans regarded the world as being made up of forms which had a much more living aspect than a comparable environment would have for us. Cornelius Osgood (1936) has suggested that the difference is comparable to walking through a field of tall grass and suddenly discovering that each blade waving in the wind is a snake. He notes that the analogy is not exact because for the Indians there would be no sense of shock. The surroundings are "alive" and this demands a respectful but not necessarily fearful attitude.

Human spirits were sometimes identified as good and bad, and among some groups there was a belief that the souls of bad Indians went to a special abode underground. In general, however, attitudes toward the afterlife seem to have been rather vague. The Indians were not particularly concerned about human spirits, nor were they afraid of them unless they lingered around a camp in the form of ghosts, in which case they were a definite source of terror.

Belief in reincarnation in human form appears to have been quite general among northern Athapaskans. Some groups believed that such reincarnations could be identified by distinguishing physical characteristics which they shared with the deceased, or by the ability to recall some event from the distant past. Among the Chandalar Kutchin, reincarnation always involved a change in sex and a shift to another family. Rebirth was particularly likely to take place when a person died young. Among some Athapaskans, it was believed that a human spirit could occasionally be reborn as an animal, but this type of metamorphosis had very restricted distribution. The Upper Tanana Indians believed that when a hunter met an animal he was unable to kill, it was an indication that he had encountered evidence of the transmigration of a human spirit into an animal form.

Perhaps the most widespread religious belief among northern Athapaskans concerned animal spirits. Myths lent sanction to attitudes about the animal world and a great deal of respect was shown at all times toward animal spirits and the power they possessed. In particular, considerable care had to be taken to avoid giving offense to such economically important animals as moose and caribou. A variety of magical practices and taboos were used to placate animal spirits and insure good hunting, some of which will be discussed later in this chapter.

One of the most interesting and widespread quasi-religious concepts among northern Athapaskans was the belief in the existence of a supernatural being or bogey man sometimes called "bush man," "brush man," or *nakhani*. This was an evil spirit who could be identified as a man, or a monster who was half man and half animal. The Upper Tanana believed that such a creature lurked in the bush around camps during the summer months awaiting a chance to steal children. Any unusual noise at night might be attributed to the bush man, and most adults could tell of some frightening experience with the creature. The Kutchin believed the *nakhani* were numerous enough to form bands and that their supernatural power permitted them to move about invisibly without the usual economic and logistic problems of the ordinary traveler.

A belief in bush men has persisted down to the present time among many Athapaskans. When I was conducting field work in the mid-1960s among the Snowdrift Chipewyan, I was frequently told about such creatures, who were said to roam the bush during the summer months, often coming close to the village. Mothers never hesitated to use the bush man to frighten children to keep them from wandering. Informants told me how the bush men wore ordinary hard-soled shoes rather than moccasins and therefore could be heard, if seldom seen, in the bush.

Among the Upper Tanana, such a quasi-religious, supernatural being has been identified in myth with an invasion from the coast. It is clear, however, that among most of the Indians, this belief is more than just a fear of invasion, and this may account for its persistence. It appears to involve a deep-rooted fear of an evil spirit, an anxiety shared by everyone. Such a concept fits readily into a belief system, the very essence of which is the placation of spirits. The widespread existence of the *nakhani* belief has also been attributed to a fear of the dangers in the woods that almost every Indian experiences at one time or another. Apparently, it is not the woods as such that are frightening, but the unknown disasters that lie within the forest depths. These could include the very real risk of becoming lost or the threat of wild animals.

Belief in and fear of a large number of spirits and supernatural beings necessitated many magico-religious practices involving the use of omens, charms, amulets, songs, and taboos. Individual, personal power was an important element in the religion and could manifest itself in numerous ways. Some individuals could foretell the future. Among the Chandalar Kutchin, for instance, the success of a forthcoming hunt was determined by means of a variation on the concept of scapulimancy, divination with the aid of an animal scapula. An arrow was burned to charcoal and then pulverized in the hand, and the ashes were then placed either on a stone scraper or a moose shoulder blade and set on fire. The fortuneteller, often an old woman, covered herself and the burning charcoal with a blanket. If she could smell burning meat, the hunt would be successful, and the pattern of the fire indicated the direction to be taken by the hunters. Scapulimancy has been described as a crude way of randomizing human behavior under conditions where avoiding fixed patterns of activity is desirable. When established methods of locating game animals have been so successful as to lead to depletion of the game supply, a device such as scapulimancy that breaks habit patterns in a more or less random fashion is of considerable value.

Animal power was most important in all the Athapaskan groups. Hunters might possess magical songs that gave them access to the power of certain animals. Usually the acquisition of animal power was intimately connected with dreams, and boys were encouraged to seek a special association with animals— which became symbols of their spiritual power—as early in life as possible.

As might be expected under circumstances where the relationship between men and animals was close and the power of animals played a major role in human well-being, animals were thought to share many human characteristics. Thus, the Great Bear Lake Indians believed that caribou and other animals had once been men, while the Dogrib believed that since both men and women could be reincarnated in animal form, animals could understand what Indians said. Many taboos were associated with the various creatures in the environment. Certain animals, such as dogs, otters, and some large birds, were never killed or eaten. Bears were almost invariably surrounded with a number of taboos that prescribed the ways in which they were to be killed and the disposal of their carcasses. Such customs hardly can be said to constitute bear ceremonialism as it is known throughout much of the boreal forest region, but they do indicate that northern Athapaskans held bears in considerable awe. Not all taboos, of course, prohibited the killing and eating of animals and, obviously, this form of complete taboo could not apply to important game animals. Nevertheless, all Athapaskans had numerous taboos of a less restrictive nature that applied to food and hunting. Nearly all of these were designed to prevent the animals' spirits from being offended and to make sure that important game remained plentiful.

In addition, there were many other restrictions related to critical periods in the life of the individual. Some of these were believed to prevent specific misfortunes, but most were observed simply because not to do so might cause bad luck—sickness, death, or lack of skill as a hunter and trapper. Although most Indians probably did not attempt to rationalize their taboos, it seems clear that restrictions and their associated rituals were related to the widely shared belief that life was threatened by evil spirits, or at least very sensitive and touchy spirits, which had to be appeased so their dangerous intentions could be forestalled. It is tempting to suggest that this preoccupation with the machinations of evil spirits was related to the ambivalent relationship between men and the game animals on which they were dependent for food.

SHAMANISM

We have noted that personal power was the vital element in religious life. Those individuals with the most personal power, the shamans, were the only professional religious practitioners. The shaman and the magico-religious practices he used to control the spirit world were the most important features of northern Athapaskan religion.

Among all the Athapaskan groups, the shaman was usually a man, but it was possible for a woman to have shamanistic power. The first sign of the calling usually came at about the age of fifteen, the neophyte shaman acquiring an animal helper or spirit in much the same manner as other individuals. However, only those persons who displayed particular skill and inclination became shamans.

It is not clear whether this modified form of vision-quest was always deliberately sought. Among the Kaska, the young person becoming a shaman would spend considerable time alone in the bush soliciting the help of an animal spirit. To the incipient Tahltan shaman, on the other hand, the spirit apparently came first in a dream, and then the neophyte went alone into the woods to solidify his relationship with the supernatural world. Among the Sekani, every youth upon reaching the age of puberty was sent out alone on a vision quest to receive his animal helper, but only a few went on to become shamans. Only occasionally did seeking a spirit helper involve the fasting and self-mutilation that was often the case with other American Indian shamans. The animal helper became the symbol of the shaman's spiritual power and, among some groups, a representation of it was always connected with shamanistic performances or seances.

A powerful shaman gradually acquired a variety of spiritual helpers upon whom he could call for assistance in performing cures and other ceremonies. A shaman might also dream of natural objects that would come to possess medicinal properties and which he would collect and keep in a small pouch on his person. The contents of this pouch symbolized his various magical powers. One such pouch belonging to a shaman of the Chandalar Kutchin contained a small ermine skin, a bear claw, and some dirt resembling wet ashes that was said to be the excrement of a large snake. Shamans also owned a number of magical songs and used drums and rattles for accompaniment when singing them. It seems certain that among most of the groups, no particular dress distinguished a shaman. However, Tanaina practitioners possessed considerable paraphernalia, including an elaborate caribou skin parka on which were sewn appendages made of claws and beaks which rattled impressively when the wearer danced. A Tanaina shaman also used drums, rattles, and masks. Shamanistic practices as a whole were most highly developed among the western Alaskan Athapaskans where Eskimo influence was strong.

The primary duties of any shaman were to prevent and cure disease. Curing usually involved the removal of a tangible object such as a stone, bullet, or piece of string, or an invisible spirit, which was considered to be the source of the patient's trouble. This concept of the intrusive nature of disease which required extraction by sucking or blowing is common to all northern Athapaskans for which data exists. It is also, of course, characteristic of American Indian shamanism generally. Prevention of disease involved frightening away the spirit through a shamanistic performance. The shaman's power actually derived from his ability to go into a trance and converse with the spirit world. Then, with the help of his particular guardian animal spirit, he could ascertain the evil spirit that was likely to have caused the patient to become ill and discourage it through a display of his power. The shaman was paid for curing by the patient or his family.

Curing was the most important shamanistic activity, but there were others. Shamans brought game to the hunters, predicted the weather, and were able to foretell the future. These are generally believed to have been communal services for which the practitioner was not paid. The ability to foretell the future was particularly valuable because the location of game could be "seen," and the strength of an enemy approaching the village or camp could be ascertained before their actual arrival. In fact, shamans appear to have assisted war parties in all the Athapaskan groups for which relevant data exists. They sometimes accompanied the party and were called upon to use their power to weaken the enemy and make the raid a success.

Hunters having poor luck frequently called for the services of a shaman to bring about a change in their fortunes. The philosophy involved was the same as that for the treatment of disease. Bad luck was believed to be caused by evil spirits and the services of a shaman were required either to forestall the activities of the evil spirits or to exorcise them.

The question of the existence of "good" and "bad" shamans is difficult to deal with in detail since much more evidence exists for the activities of the "good" practitioners. However, it is clear that shamans could also act as sorcerers and bring death or bad luck to their enemies. It was also possible for them to use black magic for their personal advantage. Even if all the shamans in a particular camp, village, or band professed to be "good," it was always possible that there were evil shamans in distant camps who were sending evil spirits to cause trouble. Thus an attempt by the "good" shaman to counteract this evil could involve a struggle between two powerful shamans conducted on the supernatural level. It was conceivable that war parties might be organized to kill the offending shaman if his wickedness was too strong for his "good" counterpart. Black magic probably existed in most of the Athapaskan groups but does not appear to have been an important activity.

This description of conventionalized shamanistic practices does little to indicate either the skill of the shaman or the colorful, mysterious nature of the abilities he possessed. Among all groups there were stories about legendary shamans, whose activities frequently reveal a good deal not only about the attitudes of people toward shamanism but also about the nature of shamanistic practice. A famous Chandalar Kutchin shaman had the color red as one of his spirit helpers and could dive into the ground and reappear wearing red clothing and carrying red objects. A common performance among the Upper Tanana was for a shaman to give a man a loaded gun and direct that he shoot him through the chest. The man with the gun fears to kill the shaman, of course, and when he finally fires, blood squirts all around, but the bullet flattens against the shaman's chest without leaving a wound. It is doubtless true that many of the descriptions of shamanistic performances in the literature have been elaborated in the telling and others may be explained simply as very clever trickery. However, it has also been suggested that evidence for telepathic and hypnotic sorcery existed among many Athapaskans, just as it is said to have existed in other areas where shamanism occurred.

CEREMONIALISM

Although dramatic group ceremonies were less prevalent among the individualistic northern Athapaskans than among some neighboring peoples, such communal ceremonies did occur. They usually involved feasting and religious elements played a part, particularly among the western groups. The potlatch may be considered such a ceremony, even though its religious elements were of minimal importance.

The Tanaina are a good example of a western group for whom feasts and ceremonies of varying degrees of complexity and duration played a major cultural role. Some of these were ordinary communal feasts of the type that took place at the time of a marriage or the completion of a major task such as the construction of a large skin boat. These ceremonies had little if any religious significance. More important from a religious standpoint was the ceremony of the first salmon, the purpose of which was to celebrate and assure the necessary supply of this important seasonal fish. It had a mythological origin and centered around the first king salmon caught each year. The fish were laid on fresh grass in front of the houses, and the people, after taking sweat baths and making other preparations, put on their best clothes to clean and cook them. Cleaning was accomplished without breaking the backbones, and the entrails were thrown back into the water. Ceremonies of a similar propitiatory nature were held at the time of killing the year's first big game. Potlatch ceremonies were also important to the Tanaina and these appear to have been considerably more complex than the ceremony previously described for the Upper Tanana.

The most elaborate ceremonies characteristic of any Athapaskan group were performed by the Ingalik in their village *kashims*. Again we find many ceremonies associated with respect for animals, including not only species important for subsistence like the salmon, but those which the Indians feared and respected because of their considerable power, such as the wolf and wolverine. A whole series of animal ceremonies were held, the major purpose of which was to insure the increase of the animal species, but which also were great social occasions providing much pleasure for the people. The major part of these ceremonies consisted of symbolic and imitative dances in the *kashim* to the accompaniment of songs and drums. The performers wore colorful masks and people attended in fine clothes. When an annual ceremony was to be given in one village, the people of other villages were welcomed, but not specifically invited. Nevertheless, there were frequently many visitors at these ceremonies, which often lasted more than two weeks.

This description provides only a modest indication of the richness of Ingalik ceremonial life, much of which, as previously noted, can hardly be called religious. Nevertheless, it is true that the important relationship between man and animals that is reflected throughout northern Athapaskan religion is a significant aspect of many of the most important Ingalik ceremonies. It should be mentioned too that the ceremonies included not only the concepts embodied in their performances, but a rich heritage of songs, dances and material culture.

It has been suggested that the rich ceremonial life of the western Athapaskans can be attributed to coastal influences or, in the case of the Ingalik, to the close proximity of riverine Eskimos. For some groups, it is apparently true that at least the ritual aspects of their ceremonial life were largely borrowed. Thus an investigator working with the Tahltan as early as 1904 noted that their feasts and dances were borrowed from the Tlingit. As for the Ingalik, the most careful research (by Osgood in the 1930s) failed to reveal satisfactory evidence of the borrowing of most ceremonies from the neighboring Eskimos. His informants believed the performances to be basically Athapaskan and he was unwilling to make a judgment either way in the matter. Regardless of the extent to which the more visible elements of ceremonies were borrowed, however, the concepts embodied in them were directly relevant to the culture of their practitioners.

NATIVISTIC MOVEMENTS

Anthropologists concerned with rapid culture change have always been interested in nativistic or religious revitalization movements. Such movements usually involve an attempt by culturally disrupted people to bring about through religious means a return to some period of their history when life was, or seemed to be, better. In its more militant form, such a movement may involve an active program for cultural transformation and revitalization. Frequently such movements are led by individuals who, having undergone a personality transformation as a result of a vision or dream, are able to communicate their revelation to the people who then become their followers.

Such movements have been described for numerous North American Indian tribes, particularly west of the Mississippi, but they are relatively unknown among northern peoples. Perhaps the best known American Indian nativistic movement was the Ghost Dance which swept the plains area of the United States and Canada during the last two decades of the nineteenth century. A variant of this movement reached the Sarsi early in the twentieth century through the Assiniboine, a neighboring plains tribe. About 1910, an Indian of the latter group named Cough Child claimed that God had been revealed to him in a vision and had instructed him to perform certain ceremonies, after which he should return to his people and restore their aboriginal religion. This was necessary because Christianity had destroyed all the power with which God had endowed them. Cough Child had the power to heal diseases and his fame spread rapidly. Although Indians from considerable distances sent for him to heal them, the Sarsi seem to have placed little credence in his mission and it died out within about ten years.

Much farther to the north, a form of messiah cult was encountered among the Great Bear Lake Indians by Cornelius Osgood (1933) at the time of his field work in that area in the late 1920s. This cult reached Great Bear Lake in the winter of 1925–1926 by way of the Dogrib. The cult activity was principally a dance that was supposed to have originated in the upper Mackenzie River region, where an Indian who suffered an epileptic fit was cured by a shaman who hit the ground with a stick and told the man to rise. The shaman became known as a messiah, although the manner in which the cult developed is not certain. It is easy, however, to discern the Christian influence in these events, an influence that is commonly present in one form or another in American Indian nativistic movements. The messiah cult was widespread among the Bear Lake and neighboring Indians at the time of Osgood's field work, but its influence did not last.

The best documented example of a nativistic movement among northern Athapaskans is provided by Robert McKennan (1965) for the Chandalar Kutchin in the community of Arctic Village. The movement centered around a former shaman whom McKennan met in 1933, but who had ceased to practice and had taught himself English by comparing a Kutchin translation of the Bible with the King James version. This individual had become converted to Christianity by arriving at the conclusion that the white man's superiority was based on his religion and his ability to write. He then attempted to learn the meaning of the Bible and during this quest for understanding, was struck by a blinding flash of light and fell unconscious. When he recovered, he believed himself to be a new man with a mission of bringing the gospel and literacy to his people. Although he preached the gospel in the normal fashion, he also attempted to persuade the people to return to reliance on their old subsistence activities. Disagreement eventually developed among the followers of this prophet and at the time McKennan met him, his influence was largely confined to his immediate family and relatives.

Students of revitalization movements recognize that the form of nativistic movement just described is one that can develop after a long period of contact between two groups that stand in an acknowledged relationship of superiority and inferiority, but where little overt domination has taken place. Although aware of Christianity and other aspects of white culture for several generations, the isolated inhabitants of Arctic Village, located well above timber line on the Chandalar River, had experienced little direct contact with outsiders and did not actually see a missionary until 1933. The movement McKennan describes, initiated by the Indians themselves, represented an attempt to combine the advantages of the white man's way of life with a vague awareness that life was probably better before he arrived.

CONCLUSION

Like their social institutions, the aboriginal northern Atha-paskan religious belief system is difficult to reconstruct in detail. Most groups have been exposed more or less continuously to mission influence since at least the middle of the nineteenth century. The nativistic movements just described are only one aspect of the reaction to culture contact in general and Christianity specifically on the part of the Indians. Although actual contacts with white missionaries were often limited to brief, widely separated visits, today virtually all Indians throughout the region profess membership in one of the Protestant denominations, or the Roman Catholic or Russian Orthodox Church. A Christian veneer covers whatever traditional beliefs remain among the various groups.

Many investigators of northern Athapaskan lifeways have noted, however, that beneath the thin layer of Christianity a surprising number of aboriginal beliefs are still strongly held. Commitment to parts of two different belief systems does not seem to concern or confuse the Indians. They are perfectly capable of seeing the two systems, Christian and traditional, as complementary rather than conflicting, a situation that may result from the fact that they do not overly concern themselves with religious problems.

It would be a mistake, however, to overemphasize this lack of interest in religion. For northern Athapaskans, as for most hunters and gatherers, the supernatural world was vague and poorly defined. Yet in those areas where the belief system touched on such significant aspects of daily life as health and illness, the weather, game control, and the prediction of things to come, it was remarkably precise and frequently complex. From this we can conclude that religion was highly functional and tended to be elaborated in those areas where the individual needed all the help he could get, including supernatural assistance. Investigators working with present-day Indians have often been able to determine the areas of importance in the diminished aboriginal belief system by noting the varying degree of emotional intensity that still surrounds them.

Chapter 5

THE INDIVIDUAL
AND HIS CULTURE

Anthropologists have found that one of the most graphic means of conveying the manner in which any sociocultural system operates is to construct a composite life cycle of a typical individual from the time he is born until he dies. Obviously life cycles are never exactly alike for any two individuals. Even in a culture that places the highest possible value on social conformity, no two persons are going to respond in the same manner to all the cultural stimuli that are presented to them. This chapter presents a single, composite northern Athapaskan life cycle, with special reference to certain elaborations that are characteristic of particular groups. Although some aspects of the individuality of growing up among a particular group of people may be obscured by this method of presentation, repetitive descriptions owing to overall similarities will be avoided. A number of consistent patterns will be noted, along with customs deeply rooted in the cultures of western and northern North America other than that of the northern Athapaskans.

The life cycle of a northern Athapaskan Indian fortunate enough to live to adulthood passed through a number of distinct phases. The individual was born into what is known as a "family of orientation." Throughout infancy and childhood he was almost completely dependent on the members of his family—his mother and father particularly, but also his older siblings and other relatives—for the warmth and security that are necessary to any individual before he can begin to make his own way in the world. This dependency decreased rapidly during adolescence. Girls were married soon after puberty, while men were usually young adults when they sought wives. When a couple married and began to have children, they established their own "family of procreation" in which they were the senior members, their children in turn becoming culturally oriented under their parental protection and care.

As in any culture, adult life was the period of an individual's greatest responsibilities during which he was required to utilize his energies and skills to the highest possible degree. In hunting and gathering societies, the demands on the resourcefulness of the individual were probably greater than in societies where the economic margin was wider and one could spend less of his time dealing with the basic problems of subsistence. The head of a northern Athapaskan family had to deal daily with the problem of providing food for his dependents. All the skills acquired from imitating his elders and from experience while he was growing up had to be brought to bear on practical problems such as the methods of hunting game and taking fish. Long range economic planning was almost impossible, the family head seldom being able to think more than a year ahead. In fact, he was usually completely occupied with activities required by the season at hand.

Although the struggle to make a living was considerable, it would be an error to represent the family head as being constantly concerned with subsistence and survival. The environment in which he lived was difficult and demanding, but not necessarily oppressive. His proven skills and abilities gave him a measure of security and his confidence grew with each succeeding demonstration of his own facility for coping with difficult problems and decisions as they arose. The northern Athapaskan family head was an individualist, even though a number of the subsistence activities in which he engaged required cooperation with others and he knew he could sometimes share in their success, skill, or simple luck. Most often his success or failure depended on his own skills, judgment, and ability.

Under ideal circumstances, the final phase of an individual's life would find him attached to a family of procreation as a secondary member. Having perhaps reached an advanced age, he would make those contributions to the welfare of the family which his restricted abilities permitted. There are indications that northern Athapaskans did not always treat the aged with respect, and when this was the case, elderly individuals may have spent some time lamenting their lost youth and physical vitality.

PREGNANCY, BIRTH, AND INFANCY

Children were greatly desired among all the Athapaskan groups and there are no indications of infanticide, except perhaps among the Bear Lake Indians where a number of historical sources reported the killing of female babies when food was scarce. Infanticide also occasionally occurred among the Ingalik, but only when a mother was unmarried or had become discouraged after giving birth to many children, all of whom died in infancy. The Bear Lake Indians obviously preferred boys, but among most groups there was no apparent preference for babies of one sex rather than the other. The Tanaina did express some preference for girls, considering them less trouble and more help to the family than boys.

During the month preceding delivery a pregnant woman was supposed to adhere to a number of food taboos, and these were likely to become more stringent as the time for birth approached. For the most part, birth took place apart from the men in a special hut or lodge erected for the purpose. Among the Upper Tanana a shallow pit was dug and lined with grass, a hut being erected over it only if the weather were cold. This special birth place did not need to be far from the family dwelling and, indeed, was sometimes only a few feet from it. Only among the Ingalik, apparently, did birth take place in the house. A thin layer of grass was spread on the bench of the dwelling and men absented themselves as the time of birth approached.

It should be emphasized that men always avoided the vicinity of a birth, the whole pattern of isolation associated with the event being related to the fact that a woman in labor was considered to be afflicted with a sickness. This sickness, the physiological process of birth itself, was likely to cause men to have poor luck or lose their skill as hunters. Similar attitudes applied to a woman during menstrual periods throughout her life. Such beliefs are widespread among hunting and gathering peoples, and it is obvious that under circumstances where skill and luck as a hunter are essential to life itself, men will consistently avoid anything they believe to have an adverse effect on their abilities.

At least one other woman, and sometimes two or three, assisted at a birth. During parturition the woman assumed a crouching or stooping position over a pit, sometimes balancing herself and assisting delivery by holding a horizontal bar lashed to a pair of uprights about three feet above the ground. In the absence of such a bar, an assistant might support her, and a second assistant, if present, would receive the child. Births were not always easy and death sometimes resulted. If a parturition proved to be particularly difficult, a shaman might be summoned to facilitate the proceedings by singing.

Following delivery, the umbilical cord was cut and the afterbirth either buried or hung in a tree deep in the woods. The Upper Tanana believed that if dogs got the afterbirth, the mother would have no more children. The use of a small section of the naval cord as an amulet to protect the life of the newborn baby was characteristic of some groups.

For a number of days after the birth of her child, the mother remained in the birth hut, and there were likely to be restrictions on her activities for as many as twenty days. Among some groups a mother was subjected to the same taboos after childbirth that accompanied female puberty. The Upper Tanana, Kutchin, and Ingalik among others adhered to taboos that were observed equally by the father and mother. An Ingalik father did no work for twenty days after the birth. During this period he wore old clothes, and when outside had to wear his parka with the hood covering his head. There were also restrictions applying to food and to sexual intercourse. The child's health and good fortune were believed to depend on the strict observance of the various taboos and restrictions.

The newborn baby was either washed or wiped clean with moss, and then wrapped in a rabbitskin robe or a moosehide bag lined with rabbitskin. Dry grass or moss was used for diapers. The small baby was frequently carried in a birch-bark cradle-chair or simply tied to the mother with a carrying strap. In this tray-like cradle or moosehide bag, the infant spent most of the first two years of its life until it was able to walk. Weaning usually did not take place until the infant was about three years old, or after another child was born. Even later weaning is frequently mentioned for northern Athapaskans, and among the Chipewyan I observed a woman offering one breast as a pacifier to a crying four- or five-year-old while nursing an infant at the other.

Naming appears to have occurred at any time during a child's early years. In some groups no particular pattern of naming was apparent, and ceremonies surrounding the event or the ownership of names were largely absent. Among the Slave, some act by the child that revealed his character was likely to result in the giving of a name, usually by the parents but sometimes by others. A child might also be named after an animal or an object. The practice of teknonymy, whereby an individual is known by the name of his son or daughter with a suffix indicating the relationship, was practiced by the Tanana and Kutchin as well as some of the Mackenzie drainage groups.

CHILDHOOD AND ADOLESCENCE

The socialization of a growing child took place largely within the immediate family; parents, grandparents, and older siblings were the most important teachers. A child who did not have a family was in a difficult situation. Orphans were usually adopted, often by a closely related family, although this did not necessarily protect them from abuse. For the most part, however, children were treated kindly, and seldom punished or forced to act against their own wishes. Information on the treatment of children, and indeed on childhood activities in general, is far from complete. In any event, corporal punishment was rare, but we can be sure that disciplinary action would occur if a child failed to adjust or was slow to take over socially approved habits.

Most authorities emphasize the importance of imitative activities in acquiring the essential adult cultural skills and moral values. Division of labor was based on sex: the men did the hunting and trapping, made tools and weapons, and drove dog teams, while women prepared game and fish for storage or consumption, gathered berries and other plant foods, tanned skins, and sewed clothing. They also carried heavy burdens while traveling and cared for children. Fishing was the one subsistence activity that engaged the efforts of both men and women.

In Athapaskan society, as among most hunting peoples, men provided most of the food. However, this statement exaggerates the inferiority of the female role. Among all the groups, women owned property in their own right, and the widespread existence of matriliny and matrilocal residence also helped to achieve a balance in the status of the sexes.

It is probable that among most groups, a boy began to accompany his father or an older brother on hunting trips while still very young. Thus a youth might be expected to have had some experience in the bush by the time he was ten or twelve years old. In some groups, a boy's first kill was marked by a small feast to which the father would proudly invite guests in honor of the youngster's achievement. The enculturation process for girls, although perhaps less spectacular, was equally important. A rather strict separation of the sexes in early childhood meant that a girl was closely associated with her mother and with household activities; she was increasingly responsible for the care of younger siblings.

Rituals at puberty varied throughout the Athapaskan area, but certain patterns are clearly discernible. Puberty rites for boys generally received little formal recognition, although this time in a young man's life was regarded as a critical period and his actions were thought to have a certain bearing on his fortunes in later life. At the very least, a boy was expected to observe minor taboos at this time. Among the Tanaina, boys of about the age of fifteen were sent into the woods for five days during which they were not to eat or drink. For a second period of five days they drank only through a bone tube, so as not to be thirsty in later life. There are also indications of a prohibition on eating and drinking after a boy killed his first large game. All of these mild activities were expected to bring a young man wealth and success.

In some groups early adolescence was associated with a modified form of the vision quest already discussed in connection with religious beliefs in which a young man sought spirit helpers and even shamanistic power. For the Kaska, this vision quest marked the completion of childhood and frequently was associated with training in hardihood and endurance. Limited puberty

rites for boys also occurred among some of the southern cordilleran groups, notably the Tahltan, Sekani, and Carrier.

Although puberty for boys may attract relatively little public
notice, a girl's first menstrual flow was a matter of community
interest because it indicated that she was ready for marriage.
From early childhood a girl was prepared by her mother and
other female relatives for what would happen to her at the time
of her first menses, and in particular she was taught the attitude
of men toward the menstruant. In some groups menstrual fluid
was believed to contain a substance that acted as a repellent to
fish and was also offensive to animals.

At the beginning of her first menstrual period a girl would
leave the camp for a special hut where she remained in complete
seclusion for a given period—among the Slave, for ten days, but
among the Upper Tanana for a month. Food and water were
brought by other women, liquids being sucked through a special
bone tube. The menstruant could not scratch herself with her
fingers, but used a special scratching stick. After the period of
seclusion, the girl might venture out occasionally, but always
with her face covered. She had to make a special effort to avoid
men, and, if the band was forced to travel at this time, she had
to break her own trail or travel in her own boat. An Upper
Tanana girl could return to her family at the end of two or three
months, but she was still regarded with some circumspection,
particularly by the men. At the conclusion of a year she was considered eligible for marriage, which took place soon after. As a
girl grew older, restrictions were a good deal less rigorous, and
she usually had to remain in seclusion only for the duration of
her menstrual period.

It is important to emphasize that throughout her life until menopause, a girl or woman, whether married or single was considered sick and unclean during her menstrual periods, a danger
both to herself and to others. Her diet was strictly limited, frequently involving a prohibition on eating fresh meat, but each
group had its own set of food taboos. Violation of such taboos
was considered harmful to the girl, but most important of all,
offensive to the animals whose flesh she ate. Thus a menstruating
woman was a danger to the survival of the group because she
had the power to reduce the subsistence abilities of the men and
to offend the spirits of game animals. It is little wonder, there-

fore, that puberty ceremonies and menstrual taboos, usually involving menstrual huts, hood-like headgear, special scratching sticks, bone drinking tubes, and taboos on fresh meat, were characteristic of all northern Athapaskan groups.

MARRIAGE

Although a girl was considered ready for marriage shortly after emerging from the seclusion related to her first menstruation, boys usually were somewhat older. The selection of a daughter's husband rested in large measure with her family, particularly her mother and other female relatives. It was natural that the girl's parents would look with favor on an older and wealthy suitor. In any event, arranged marriages were the rule and those based on individual choice, while they did occur, were often believed to be less successful. Since polygyny occasionally occurred in some Athapaskan groups, it was sometimes the case that older men had several wives while younger men were unable to find any. Polyandrous marriages are reported for the Kaska in which the husbands were always brothers. Such arrangements were restricted, however, to old men unable to hunt sufficiently to support their families.

Information concerning forms of preferential marriage is limited, and it is not always possible to determine whether the incomplete data available applies to the aboriginal period. The Slave are reported to have preferred marriages between parallel cousins and the Upper Tanana between cross cousins. [A cross cousin is the child of a father's sister or mother's brother. Children of a father's brother or mother's sister are technically known as parallel cousins.] Among the Tanaina and Ingalik incest rules were extended in principle if not in practice to include all cousins. Upper Tanana marriages were exogamous between phratries; the prospective Tanana bridegroom had to choose from the marriageable girls of the opposite moiety either in his own or another village. Matrilineal moieties among the Kaska were also exogamous.

A period of bride service, sometimes as long as two years, was characteristic of most Athapaskan groups. Among the Kaska, much of this service took place before the couple was actually considered married, although it is clear that the prospective groom enjoyed sexual relations with the girl during this period. More commonly the period of bride service took the form of temporary matrilocal residence, the young family having the right to live apart from the parents of either spouse once the groom's obligations were fulfilled. It seems clear that the tendency toward matrilocal residence reported so frequently for northern Athapaskan groups was associated with some form of bride service. Under whatever circumstances it occurred, such an arrangement allowed a young man to demonstrate his capacity as a provider and worker to the satisfaction of his wife's or prospective wife's parents.

Ideally, marriages were supposed to be permanent, but in fact divorces occurred frequently, although apparently with greater ease among some groups than in others. In some, the power of public opinion could inhibit divorce to a certain extent. If a man divorced his wife, the news spread rapidly, and as a result he might experience some difficulty in obtaining another mate. It is also true that divorce was much rarer after the birth of children.

OLD AGE AND DEATH

Although in many cultures old age is a time when the individual enjoys the respect and deference owing to his long years of experience, this does not seem to have been the case among northern Athapaskans. In a demanding natural environment where subsistence activities were sometimes hazardous, many individuals did not live to see old age. Those who did frequently found their declining years burdened not only with waning physical abilities, but also with the disappearance of whatever prestige they might have enjoyed during their more robust years. A woman frequently associated menopause with the onset of old age, while a man realized that the respect and prestige which accrued to him through his success as a hunter would disappear with his diminishing skill at subsistence activities.

In some cases, however, lack of respect and honor for the aged seems to have gone farther than a simple withdrawal of prestige from those members of the group who could no longer bear children or support themselves and their dependents. Historical sources report that when Chipewyan men and women became too old to work, they were treated with overt disrespect, an attitude that seems to have continued to the present day. During my field work among the Chipewyan, I frequently noted that young people made disrespectful comments about and to elderly individuals, physical defects in the aged also inspiring scornful remarks. It sometimes appeared to me that any living thing, even a dog, was an object of scorn if it were old. Among the Chandalar Kutchin, however, old people enjoyed high status because their long experience was considered to give them superior wisdom.

Since Restricted Wanderers were almost continually on the move from one hunting or fishing location to another, they could make little provision for those who were unable to keep up. Thus abandonment of the aged was widespread. An early historical source estimated that one-half the elderly Chipewyans of both sexes perished in this manner, and a somewhat later observer was under the impression that abandonment of the aged occurred with greater frequency among the Chipewyan than among the Eskimo.

Some of the southern cordilleran groups were also well known for this practice. Aged and infirm Sekani dropped by the way to die of starvation. Their kinsmen built them good shelters and left what food and fuel they could spare before departing hastily to lessen the grief of farewells. Among the Kaska, very old people were sometimes abandoned in the autumn, alongside a fire with a large pile of wood. Later in the winter, relatives would return to bury the bodies. A similar practice is reported for the Slave, yet in both groups it was not uncommon for the aged, like the blind and otherwise infirm, to be pulled along on a toboggan as the rest of the band moved from place to place. It is probably true, therefore, that abandonment of the aged and sick, though frequent among some groups, was resorted to only when the young and vigorous themselves appeared to be in danger during an extended period of game shortage.

The actual approach of death was fatalistically greeted in most cases, although considerable variation with reference to this very individual experience is to be expected. The Upper Tanana are said to have awaited death with equanimity, while among the Slave it was regarded with considerable apprehension. In all groups, however, death was an event that was socially significant and its impact was strongly felt, often over a long period of time.

Since in any society the individual's role is closely linked with those of his fellow members, the death of any person sets in motion a series of events aimed in various ways at restoring the social equilibrium.

Death was generally recognized as involving the loss of the spirit or shadow. All tribes for which data is available recognized some forms of death as "natural." Suicides, which occurred infrequently, and accidents such as drowning were considered due to natural causes. Death in childbirth, starvation, and murder were similarly understood. However, it is likely that many deaths were attributed to malevolent magic, and that even persons who died naturally might have been considered vulnerable as a result of sorcery.

Immediately following death, the corpse was dressed in new clothes made especially for the occasion, frequently in advance if death was anticipated. Among the Chandalar Kutchin, a deceased man's face was washed and painted in red and black with the designs he had used in life. His dwelling was torn down and his widow and relatives, together with friends, singed their hair and wailed in mourning around a special fire built for the occasion. The Upper Tanana removed the deceased through the smoke hole of the lodge so that the evil spirit which caused the death would not find its way back to the camp. The tent or lodge, however, was apparently not destroyed. Singing the hair as a sign or mourning was particularly common among Athapaskans. Among the Tanaina, it was accompanied by other forms of self-mutilation, particularly by widows.

Except for immediate relatives, mourning was usually restrained and highly ritualized. Those who actually performed the work involved in a burial frequently had to observe numerous and demanding taboos over a long period of time. Among the Chandalar Kutchin, this work was performed by members of a sib other than that of the deceased, and they were rewarded for their efforts with gifts from the dead man's relatives. However, they were subject to a series of restrictions for a period of two or three weeks following the funeral and could not return to their own lodges. Even after returning, they could not have intercourse with their wives for an additional number of weeks.

The dead were disposed of in four ways: by cremation, inhumation, abandonment, and caching in a tree. Cremation may have been the oldest and most widespread method, since it is described for the Upper Tanana, Chandalar Kutchin, Tanaina, Ingalik, Kaska, and Sekani, among others. However, cremation was probably the exclusive method of disposal only for the Tanaina. Among the Kaska, members of the opposite moiety built a coffin of lashed poles to contain dry wood along with the body. The workers then struck a fire and departed, nobody actually witnessing the cremation. Later the remains were raked together and buried on the spot.

The most elaborate forms of inhumation were found among the Ingalik, where the type of burial frequently depended on the wealth of the deceased. Coffin burial was most desirable, the coffin being placed on a rack at the edge of the cemetery until either the spring or fall burial season, then deposited in a coffin house in the cemetery. This type of burial involved an elaborate ceremony in the *kashim*. For those whose relatives could not afford a coffin burial, disposal usually consisted of simple interment in the ground.

Platform burial was known in such widely separated groups as the Sekani and Kutchin. Among the former, it was a method reserved for persons of distinction. The Kutchin apparently did not practice this form of burial until after the introduction of the steel axe, when platforms could be constructed more easily. Raised burials were also common among the Slave.

It is unlikely that abandonment of the dead was an accepted pattern of behavior among any of the Athapaskan groups, although it sometimes occurred. Kaska men killed in warfare were left where they fell, and for all groups, in times of starvation the survivors were often too weak to dispose of the dead.

Placing property or food with a corpse was occasionally practiced. Among the Chandalar Kutchin, tools, weapons, snowshoes, and dentalium shells were placed with the body. A dying Ingalik could indicate whether he wished his property burned, buried with him, or distributed among his friends. A common feature of Athapaskan cemeteries is a grave house placed above the interred body, and among the Ingalik, as we have noted, the coffin is actually placed in the grave house. It is probable that the coffin house had its origin on the northwest coast, where it contained the ashes of the deceased, and some Athapaskans, such as the Tahltan and the Carrier, used it in that manner. Among other groups, particularly those of the northern cordilleran region, a coffin house was simply constructed over the grave and occasionally contained belongings of the deceased.

THE LIFE CYCLE SINCE EUROPEAN CONTACT

Many of the beliefs and practices that characterized the life cycle of northern Athapaskan Indians during aboriginal times are either no longer carried out, or exist only in greatly attenuated form. Since some of the beliefs and their associated practices impinged in various ways on modern attitudes toward health and hygiene, they have been discontinued as a result of efforts by the American and Canadian governments to provide better health education and care to people living in remote, rural areas. Others have declined or disappeared in conjunction with the general decline of the aboriginal belief system.

Typical of the changes that have affected various stages of the life cycle are those that have occurred in the practices surrounding childbirth. At the time of my field work among the Snowdrift Chipewyan, births were taken very much for granted and a minimum of disturbance in the family pattern of living was caused by the arrival of a new child. A public health nurse made periodic visits to the community and encouraged women to abandon the traditional position for delivery. Expectant mothers took no particular precautions and there was no apparent concern over an approaching birth. There were no dietary restrictions and the mother continued her usual chores right up until labor began. Pregnant women usually went to Yellowknife to have their babies delivered in the government hospital, by arrangement with the Indian and Northern Health Services nurse. Those who preferred to give birth in the village were attended by midwives who had received some instruction in elementary hygiene from the nurse. All this is in marked contrast to the traditional attitudes toward birth among the Chipewyan, which were similar to those discussed earlier for Athapaskans in general. Similar circumstances exist at the present time among other groups where contemporary studies have been made, and it is clear that 150 years of Euro-American contact together with intensive efforts in the field of public health over the past twenty years have eliminated traditional attitudes to a large degree.

It is probably safe to say that in no Athapaskan group do girls any longer go into seclusion at puberty, and this practice may have been in decline for as long as fifty years. It is also probable, however, that some of the other taboos associated with first menstruation are still observed. Among the Chandalar Kutchin, for example, those taboos involving food and the handling of freshly killed animals are still observed and any neglect of them is believed to bring bad luck to the husband. As recently as the 1930s, an Upper Tanana girl at the time of her first menstruation lived in a corner of the tent partitioned off by a blanket.

Traditional Indian names are still used, but it is likely that all Athapaskan Indians today have Christian names, many of Biblical origin, reflecting the presence of Christian missions throughout the area. The first missionaries gave the Snowdrift Chipewyan Christian first names only. Since the missionaries were Oblates, the names were usually French, and they still are at the present time. The general use of family names seems to have begun at the time of first contacts with the Canadian government, when it became necessary for the various members of a family to be readily identifiable for maintaining accurate band lists and other government records. Certain individuals took the names of Euro-Canadians in the area, or of geographical locations, while others used French and English translations of their Chipewyan names.

The replacement of aboriginal marriage patterns by Christian practices has been noted. Polygyny has completely disappeared, and girls are now somewhat older at the time of marriage than they were in aboriginal times. The number of intermarriages between members of the various Athapaskan groups has increased as the isolation of some groups has broken down and increasing numbers of Indians move to urban or trading centers.

Cremation of the dead disappeared with the coming of the white man. Within historic times, inhumation has become the accepted means of disposal and Christian cemeteries are a characteristic feature of every contemporary Athapaskan community. Most other traditions and ceremonies associated with death have either disappeared or been greatly modified, and ideas about death and afterlife held by the Indians are likely to be simplified versions of those preached by clergymen of the various Christian denominations with whom the Indians have been in contact.

ATHAPASKAN PERSONALITY: SPECULATIONS

The limited literature on culture and personality among northern Athapaskans suggests a number of motivational trends that presumably have their roots in the life cycle of the individual. There is some indication that contemporary northern Athapaskans possess a conflicting set of value orientations: the individual is confronted with traditional stimuli to be a self-sufficient person, able to deal successfully with the problems confronting him during his life time, and at the same time to be dependent on others for the solution of his problems. John Honigmann, in his studies of Kaska personality, traces the origin of this conflict to the early and progressively more intensive rejection of the child by his parents. Immediately following infancy, the Kaska child develops a sense of youthful responsibility, independence, and self-reliance. Correlated with this early development of independence, however, is a syndrome of anxiety about the possibility of achieving significant goals. Examples of dependence are difficult to reconstruct for the aboriginal period, but according to Honigmann (1949), they are easily discernible in the continued subordination, including care by the superior (Euro-Canadian government officials, traders, etc.), that has characterized the contact period.

The explanation for the conflict inherent in this personality pattern among Athapaskans is doubtless rooted in child training techniques and experiences, but adult experiences also play a role in maintaining psychological characteristics. It can be suggested, for example, that most Athapaskan Indians are intimately concerned (although perhaps below the level of consciousness) with man's place in a harmonious natural environment. A significant factor is man's friendly, kin-like relationship to animals, which, by tradition and necessity, he is forced to kill. Although it is not necessary to see guilt in this ambivalent situation, as has been suggested for some Eskimo groups, there was doubtless considerable anxiety over what was, after all, a situation involving forced hostility. To people concerned with their role in a harmonious universe, it is expected that man should be controlled by his world and should attempt to control it in more or less equal part, always balancing action through self-assertion with

the necessity of adjusting to rules and to the rigors of an environment that no person can hope even partially to master.

There is a second explanation that appears to have some merit.
The few studies that have been made indicate northern Athapaskans to be or at least to have a desire to be strongly self-
sufficient, since their cultural values point very much in this direction. However, the rigors of the environment make if always
possible that they may become helpless and dependent. Further-
more, they are aware that dependency in old age is a very real
possibility. These factors, together with a stringent rejection of
childhood dependency by the parents, give them unconscious
dependency strivings.

It should be emphasized that this discussion is highly specula-
tive, the second explanation in particular being based on relatively little information concerning aboriginal Athapaskan child-
rearing practices. What is more, it is unlikely that we will ever
know much more about these practices, although their general
outlines can be discerned through the study of contemporary
people. The fact that studies show an increase in Athapaskan
dependency in the contact period may have an ecological explanation. The contemporary Indian may experience an increase
in apathy resulting from continuous frustration in the contact
situation. Thus Indians have come to accept the fact that they are
more acted upon by their twentieth century world than they are
able to act on it. They are inclined to feel that their attempts to
affect their environment are more likely to fail than to succeed.
Thus they are increasingly willing to accept passively whatever
happens to them. The contemporary Athapaskan can thus be said
increasingly to be placed in a passively acceptant relation to life
by the bewildering nature of the contact environment.

Chapter 6

THE HISTORY OF THE EUROPEAN CONTACT

The term "contact" in the title of this chapter refers to a particular time when northern Athapaskan Indians began to react and adapt to elements of the white man's culture and to those individuals who introduced them. For most of this period, whites and Indians were in direct contact with one another and their interactions were thus based on face-to-face relations. During the earliest years of the period under consideration, however, the European cultural presence made itself felt before direct contact took place. A number of groups, particularly in the Mackenzie drainage and along the Pacific coast, came to rely on items of European material culture considerably in advance of their initial contact with white men.

A significant factor in the history of white contact throughout the western subarctic is that the inhabitants, except in a few limited instances, did not wage war with European intruders, nor were they forcibly removed from their lands. The climate and geography of the subarctic are such that the region had little appeal to settlers of the type who took over the lands of Indians throughout much of North America. Livestock raising and farming are possible only in limited areas at the southern extremities of the region occupied by northern Athapaskans.

The most important resource of the region from the white man's standpoint was fur, and this significant product could be obtained most efficiently by the aboriginal inhabitants themselves. Those whites who did settle permanently in the area did so as trappers competing with the Indians and, to a large extent, sharing their way of life. Only in the past few decades have Canadian and American economic activities intruded on areas occupied by northern Athapaskans. Mining, lumbering, fishing, and other extractive industries still utilize only very limited portions of the region.

The western subarctic was penetrated from two directions by representatives of European nations. From the east came the English fur traders. Having secured their position in eastern Canada, they followed the continental rivers and lakes to the interior of the Canadian northwest, where trading posts were established in the drainage of the Mackenzie River in the late eighteenth century. From the west came the Russians, who, after 1741, explored the coast and ascended the major rivers into the interior. Trading posts had been established among the Alaskan Athapaskans by 1840. The fur trade did not bring about rapid change, but it is possible to discern two major phases of contact relations: the period of early contact, and a later period when the fur trade was fully established and the influence of Christian missionaries became a factor in the changing conditions of life for northern Athapaskans.

EARLY CONTACT PERIOD (1700–1850)

Goods offered by the Europeans invariably reached native groups before the traders themselves appeared on the scene, since Indians in direct contact with traders served as middlemen for groups further removed from the trading centers. These middlemen made a considerable profit on the implements and other goods that passed through their hands in exchange for furs. It is not difficult to imagine that traditional enmities were exacerbated and new ones developed as various Indian groups struggled to secure favorable positions with reference to trade. But whatever the circumstances and wherever the location, the demand for trade goods on the part of the Indians never faltered. Iron chisels, knives, and axes, the earliest and most basic trade goods, were vastly superior to any implements which the Indians made from traditional materials. Knowledge of these miraculous metal tools and their many uses spread throughout northwestern North America well ahead of their purveyors, just as the implements themselves eventually did.

Trading posts located along the west coast of Hudson Bay provided the first trade goods to reach the Canadian northern Athapaskans. Few details are known concerning the manner in which these materials reached Indians who had yet to see a white man. There are indications that some of the eastern Chipewyan were receiving English trade goods by 1700, having obtained them from the Cree who were in direct contact with a post at York Factory at the southern end of Hudson Bay. In 1717 the Hudson's Bay Company established a post at the mouth of the Churchill River for the express purpose of encouraging the "Northern Indians," as Athapaskans were known in the early days of the fur trade, to trade their furs directly rather than through the Cree. The Chipewyan, supplied with firearms, not only freed themselves of their dependence on the Cree, but drove the Eskimos north and oppressed the Yellowknife and Dogrib by preventing them from making the trip to the trading post and forcing them to exchange their furs for only a small part of their actual value in European goods. This situation was unsatisfactory to the Hudson's Bay Company, and one of the purposes of Samuel Hearne's monumental overland trip to the Coppermine River in 1771–1772 was to bring the "Far Indians," as those Athapaskans northwest of Chipewyan territory were called, into the trade at Churchill. It was believed that if direct contact could be established with these Indians, new incentives to receive trade goods would bring about more intensive trapping.

Following the explorations of Hearne, attention began to be centered on the northwest as a potentially fertile field for the development of the fur trade. For nearly a century after its establishment in 1670, the Hudson's Bay Company had maintained only coastal posts with the idea that Indians would be drawn there to trade. However, in the last quarter of the eighteenth century this policy was circumvented by "free-traders" who went inland with canoes and intercepted the Indians to trade with them before they reached the coastal posts. In 1778 a number of traders in the Saskatchewan country pooled their resources and dispatched Peter Pond into the northern interior. He established a post near Lake Athabasca and spent the winter trading with the Cree and Chipewyan. The extension of the fur trade to Great Slave Lake took place shortly thereafter.

Following the success of Pond, an enterprising group of Montreal traders formed the Northwest Company, which constructed a post near the mouth of the Slave River in 1786. In response to these developments, the Hudson's Bay Company was forced to extend its activities into the interior, and they built a post on Great Slave Lake at about the same time. This pattern of the establishment of parallel posts also occurred on Lake Athabasca, where Fort Chipewyan was built in 1788 by the Northwest Company and the nearby Fort Wedderburne by the Hudson's Bay Company shortly thereafter.

The intense rivalry between these two companies had unfortunate effects on the Indians. Alcohol was used as an inducement to trade, and the intensity of competition resulted in the early depletion of the beaver population in some areas. These circumstances did not affect the Athapaskans of the far northwest, however, for north of the area occupied by the Chipewyan there were few direct confrontations between rival traders.

A far more destructive consequence of the European presence among Athapaskans and neighboring peoples in the early contact period was the introduction of European-derived diseases such as influenza, tuberculosis, and smallpox. In 1781 a severe smallpox epidemic struck the Chipewyan, and the explorer Samuel Hearne estimated that as much as 90 percent of the total population died. Diseases and related periods of starvation continued to reduce the population of this group, which bore the brunt of the earliest Athapaskan contact with Europeans. In 1862, there were said to be 900 Chipewyan trading into Fort Chipewyan, but by 1879 there were only 537.

In 1821 an abrupt end came to the fur trade rivalry in the Canadian northwest when the Hudson's Bay Company absorbed the Northwest Company. An effective trade monopoly was thus established that stretched from Hudson Bay to the Mackenzie River and from the Arctic coast to the plains of Manitoba and Saskatchewan. This important event brought to a close the period of early contact east of the Rocky Mountains.

Trading posts in northeastern Siberia were the source of the first European manufactures to reach northern Athapaskans from the west. These Russian posts had been established by the late eighteenth century, and European goods began to flow into Alaska from the Chukchee and Siberian Eskimos by way of inhabitants of the Diomede Islands and settlements on Seward Peninsula. Annual Eskimo trade fairs on the Alaskan coast became important distribution centers, not only for the Eskimos of southwestern Alaska and the Yukon and Kuskokwim regions, but also for Athapaskans in the latter areas.

Following the Russian discovery of Alaska in 1741, fur hunters began to exploit areas of the north Pacific where fabulous riches in furs had been reported. Some of these hunters reached Kodiak Island as early as 1762. Up to this time, fur gathering had been in the hands of individual entrepreneurs, but in 1781, a well-organized company of eastern Siberian merchants began to exploit the American fur trade. By the end of the eighteenth century, this company was able to overcome its rivals for control, and under the name of the Russian-American Company, it became established as a state monopoly by imperial decree in 1799.

In the late eighteenth century, prior to the establishment of the Russian-American Company, competition between various Russian trading companies was centered in the Cook Inlet region. A highlight of this period was the founding of Nikolayevskiy Redoubt at the site of the present-day village of Kenai in 1793. During approximately the same period, British explorers, notably Captain James Cook, Captains Nathaniel Portlock and George Dixon, and Captain George Vancouver, visited and traded with the coastal Tanaina.

Early in the nineteenth century, as the number of fur-bearing animals declined in the traditionally exploited areas of southeastern Alaska, the Russian-American Company was forced to turn its attention to the vast area of southwestern Alaska north of the Alaska Peninsula. This was an unknown region in which it was hoped that new profits could be reaped through trade with the Eskimo and Indian inhabitants for beaver pelts. After initial explorations, a post, Mikhailovskiy Redoubt, was established north of the mouth of the Yukon in 1883. The way was then open for Russian penetration of the Yukon region and the expansion of the fur trade to the Ingalik and Koyukon Indians.

In the Prince William Sound region, the Russians had established themselves at the mouth of the Copper River by 1800 and explored sections of the river between 1820 and 1850. However, they were never able to reach its headwaters. Coastal shipping trade during the late eighteenth and early nineteenth centuries aided the Tlingit in establishing extensive trade relations with Athapaskans living in the southern cordilleran region, who supplied these coastal peoples with furs in exchange for trade items.

In both the eastern and western areas of the Athapaskan subarctic, European contact with the native inhabitants was determined to a large extent by geography. In the west, the north Pacific allowed the earliest explorers and traders access to the immediate vicinity of Athapaskan territory, while the river systems of southeastern and southwestern Alaska made penetration of the interior regions relatively easy. In the east, an extensive series of connected waterways provided rapid movement through the interior even though considerable distances were involved. In fact, only the mountain chains separating the arctic from the Pacific drainage constituted a meaningful barrier to European exploration and the establishment of trade in the western subarctic. This barrier was particularly significant in the north, where the rugged mountainous country and the long river trips necessary to reach it left the native peoples relatively isolated from direct contact with Europeans until quite late in the historic period, well past the period of early contact in other areas.

Relations between Indians and Europeans in the period of early contact tended to be somewhat different east of the Rocky Mountains than in areas to the west. The Chipewyan, Beaver, and Yellowknife were the first groups contacted, and they quickly obtained firearms either from their Algonkian neighbors or directly from Europeans. With this advantage over other Athapaskans, they were able to disrupt traditional demographic alignments throughout the upper Mackenzie drainage area. There was, however, no initial hostility between whites and Indians, and thus no attempts to prevent traders from establishing posts in particular areas, even though the location of these posts frequently disturbed the middleman relationship enjoyed by the most eastern groups.

Along the archipelago and throughout southeastern Alaska the situation was somewhat different. The Russians, fresh from their subjugation of the inhabitants of the Aleutian Islands, reacted violently to resistance from coastal peoples like the Tlingit and Tanaina and from riverine groups such as the Koyukon and Atna.

The unstable conditions on the coast resulted partly from the warlike nature of peoples such as the Tlingit, and partly from the Russian practice of organizing parties of Indians for sea otter hunts. These Indians were frequently away from home for long periods of time and were treated harshly by the Russians; in fact, hostages were often taken from among the families of the hunters in order to insure their good behavior. In general, the Alaskan Indian populations were more resistant to the Russians than the Athapaskans of the east ever were to the English. The Russians, however, gradually learned from experience and were more circumspect in their relations with the Indians of southwestern Alaska than they had been in the southeastern area. Nevertheless, incidents of high-handed behavior on the part of traders and the tendency of the Indians to blame the Russians for epidemics and other misfortunes occasionally led to bloodshed.

Inter-Indian aggression occasionally occurred in the west, but apparently with less frequency than in the east. In the southern cordilleran area the coastal Tlingit fought with the Tsetsaut and the Sekani also engaged in warfare with coastal peoples. The general lack of hostilities in this region can probably be explained by the contrasting environments of the coastal and inland zones. The less demanding coastal environment made it unlikely that the peoples of this area would wish to take over territory from the inland mountain peoples. Rather, they were content to establish a trading dominance, which proved to be significant in the acceptance of many northwest coast cultural traits by people in the southern cordilleran region in the early contact period. In southwestern Alaska, the network of major rivers and their tributaries gave all people virtually equal access to the Russian trading posts so that no single group could successfully establish itself as middleman and thus control the access of others to trade goods.

THE STABILIZED FUR TRADE AND MISSION PERIOD (1850–1940)

In the western subarctic, the period of stabilized fur trade was long, a time of relatively slow, uninterrupted change. Contact with whites was channeled through a few representatives of the trading companies and the church. It should be emphasized that such contacts were relatively infrequent and that although Indian lifeways were gradually altered, most of the Indians went about their activities without encountering whites. Despite the seeming slowness of change and the relative infrequency of direct contact, however, throughout the stabilized fur trade and mission period the Indian standard of living continually shifted toward greater and greater dependence on items of European manufacture.

The existence of a network of established trading posts throughout the northern Athapaskan area meant that the Indians had regular access to trade goods. This access, however, was directly dependent upon the ability of the Indians to produce furs. When trading monopolies existed, as was the case in the Canadian northwest until after 1900 and in Alaska until at least 1880, credit relationships grew up between the Indians and the posts where they regularly traded their furs. As a creditor, the Indian's economic horizon was theoretically narrowed, but since competition did not exist, his relationship with the trader was stable. It was essential that the trader give credit in order to receive fur; a trapper not working his trapline because he could not obtain credit was certainly of no value to the trader.

Although bound to a particular trading post as a result of this economic relationship, all Athapaskans were free on the land. This situation was essential to the interests of the fur trade, but the Indian's mobility was reduced as he became increasingly dependent on the post as the source of material goods which began as luxuries but increasingly became necessities. Wild game and fish continued to be important for subsistence, although in some areas, particularly in the west, European foods were introduced as early as the 1880s. Aboriginal clothing disappeared rapidly, since traders wishing to discourage the Indians from using valuable furs for clothing carried European clothing and cloth at low prices. Some items of traditional Indian material culture, particularly those associated with housing and transportation, continued to be made from local materials until relatively recent times. But the tools and implements used to process the natural materials were derived almost exclusively from the trader.

As noted previously, in some areas occupied by northern Athapaskans the early contact period began much later than in others.

This was particularly true for those people inhabiting the region between the Continental Divide and the Pacific coastal ranges. It was not until 1847 that the Hudson's Bay Company expanded into the Yukon drainage, with the establishment of Fort Yukon in the region occupied by the Kutchin. In the following year Fort Selkirk was built in Tutchone country. In establishing these interior posts, the Hudson's Bay Company hoped to be able to compete effectively with the coastal traders who were being supplied with furs by Tlingit middlemen. The eastern Kutchin, Han, some Tanana, and probably the southeastern Koyukon were able to establish direct contact with the traders at Fort Yukon. The existence of Fort Selkirk greatly annoyed the Tlingit whose position as middlemen in the trade was threatened. They destroyed it in 1852, and until the gold rush of 1898, a virtual blockade existed by means of which the Tlingit prevented traders from entering the upper Yukon country. It was almost the beginning of the twentieth century before such groups as the Upper Tanana, Tutchone, and Tahltan had direct contact with traders in their own territory.

The missionization of Athapaskan populations was, generally speaking, a feature of the stabilized fur trade period. Russian Orthodox missionaries, representatives of the official government church whose activities were always closely associated with those of the Russian-American Company, were earliest on the scene and began to convert the Tanaina in 1794. However, Russian missionary efforts were thwarted by the hostility that existed between the two peoples. In fact, an attempt by the mission at Nikolayevskiy Redoubt to reach the interior Tanaina resulted in the murder of a priest, Father Juvenal, in 1796.

The Russian church did not extend its activities north of the Alaska Peninsula until the 1830s, when from a mission station on the lower Yukon River established in 1836 or 1837 they converted the Ingalik and perhaps some of the Koyukon. Their inland influence was not extensive, however, and in terms of the total Athapaskan population of the Russian-influenced area, the number of Indians successfully converted was not great. Following the purchase of Alaska by the United States in 1867, Roman Catholic and various Protestant denominations moved into the area, and by 1900, virtually all Alaskan Athapaskans were at least nominal Christians.

The Russian Orthodox Church and the Russian-American Company expanded together in Alaska, but in the eastern Athapaskan area, the Hudson's Bay Company was determined to prevent the Indians from being exposed to any aspect of European culture that did not contribute to their proficiency as fur trappers. Therefore, it was only after 1850 that Canadian Athapaskans were directly exposed to missionary influence. Members of the French-speaking Roman Catholic Oblate Order were the most energetic proselytizers, and although Anglican missionaries made some converts, the Catholic faith became dominant among Canadian Athapaskans.

The first Oblates arrived in Canada in 1845 and two years later reached the Athapaskan area. A mission was established at Fort Chipewyan in 1851, and in 1857 missionaries penetrated the western Slave area, reaching Fort Simpson. By 1868 a mission had been founded at Fort Nelson. Most Athapaskans in the northern cordilleran area and arctic drainage lowlands were quickly converted, but in the southern cordilleran there was some resistance. By 1900 all Indians in northwest Canada except those in the most isolated settlements were nominal Christians. It is worth noting, however, that some settlements did not actually see a missionary until somewhat later. The Chandalar Kutchin, for example, were exposed to Christianity after the establishment of an Anglican mission at Fort Yukon in 1861. However, the residents of Arctic Village on the remote upper Chandalar did not actually receive a visit from a missionary until 1933.

The Russian Orthodox Church in Alaska and the Anglican and Roman Catholic churches in Canada established mission schools, but these appear to have had a minimal effect on Indian children. The Russian schools were located in trading centers and the students were mostly children of mixed-blood post employees. Mission schools operated by the Roman Catholic and Protestant churches both in Canada and Alaska were equally ineffective in serving a large proportion of the school-age children. Only a very small number actually received an education and most of those eventually returned to their homes and a more or less traditional Indian life. Although the United States government assumed responsibility for the education of some native children in Alaska before 1900, the effectiveness of educational programs was not noticeably increased.

Students of Athapaskan culture have noted that the dominant forces of acculturation influencing northern Athapaskans, the church and the fur trade, were two separate systems forced by circumstances to work together, but with little in common. Often antagonism existed between the trader and the missionary, a situation that was made worse in northwestern Canada by the fact that the trader was frequently an Anglo-Saxon Protestant and the missionary a French Roman Catholic. The two institutions had vastly different goals and competed with each other in an attempt to manipulate the Indians for their own ends.

Traders and missionaries were attracted to the western subarctic because of the Indian inhabitants and were dependent on them to achieve their goals. Beginning in the 1860s, however, some areas of Athapaskan territory, notably northern British Columbia and the upper Yukon River region, were the focus of an influx of whites that was not related in any way to the aboriginal inhabitants. These were gold miners and homesteaders who expected to exploit the environment by methods that were unknown to the Indians. Such developments were in marked contrast to the fur trade, which was dependent on the Indians and on modified traditional subsistence activities. Whereas the Indians were at the very center of the fur trade, even if almost totally ignorant of the mechanisms affecting the value of the furs they traded, they were peripheral to the settlements established for homesteading and mining activities. It is important to emphasize that these settlements, unlike the trading posts, were white-oriented and provided services primarily for whites. Indians might provide some useful goods and services to the whites, but they were not essential to their operations. For example, miners coming into the upper Yukon country in 1898 generally brought their own supplies or were supplied by traders in the area. Nevertheless, they frequently purchased dried fish and fresh meat from the Indians, and the latter also cut wood for steamboats, the main source of river transportation during that period.

June Helm has recently proposed the term "boom frontier" to distinguish the type of intrusion into a region characterized by an initial large white population which quickly diminished or moved to another location following shifting economic opportunities. The most notable boom frontier occurred in the upper Yukon drainage, but little trace of the great activity of the gold rush now remains.

In marked contrast are the "settled frontiers" which exist in areas of northern Athapaskan territory suitable for farming and ranching. A stable white population has largely displaced Indians in the valleys of the Peace, Frazier and Tanana rivers. Those most affected by settled frontiers were the Chilcotin, Carrier, Tahltan, and Beaver in the southern cordilleran area and the Tanaina and Tanana in Alaska. To a large extent, these peoples have been driven from their lands and relegated to the same minority status that Indians in other areas of North America have been experiencing for a much longer period.

CHANGES IN INDIAN ADAPTATION

In the early contact period the Indians obtained more efficient tools and utensils in exchange for the furs they trapped. Luxury items and food products do not appear to have been important items of trade during this period. Nevertheless, Athapaskan lifeways began to change in some essential ways.

Trapping is essentially an individual activity, and although a trapper may work with one or more partners, the traps he sets are his own, as are the proceeds from the skins that he trades. We have noted that individualism was a significant aspect of Athapaskan adaptation, and thus the introduction of commercial trapping did not create as much disruption as it might in a culture that stressed communal subsistence activities. Those cooperative pursuits that did exist, such as the caribou drive, declined in importance, and some changes in patterns of sharing also occurred, but the sharing of big game and other important resources in the environment, a deeply rooted concept in traditional Athapaskan culture, has continued to be significant.

Aboriginal subsistence activities did not involve extensive trapping and most of the furbearing animals desired by the fur trade were not suitable for food. Only the beaver was important aboriginally as a source of both food and skins for clothing. It was the need to procure food to support life during periods when animals without food value were being hunted that eventually bound the Indians closely to the posts where they traded.

Trapping effectively signaled the end to exploitation of the total environment. Specialized knowledge of animal behavior was still an important adaptive strategy, but its emphasis shifted considerably. Knowledge of the habits of furbearing animals and their environment was now of greater importance than a similar knowledge of large game animals and fish. This shift of emphasis and its commercial implications also disturbed the balanced reciprocal relationship between the hunter and his animal spirit helpers, thus undermining a basic aspect of the traditional religious belief system.

During the stabilized fur and mission period, earlier trends were simply increased and intensified. The Indians became more heavily dependent on trade goods, and firearms began to play a more important part in all types of subsistence activities. Steel traps, however, do not appear to have been a significant factor in commercial trapping until after 1900. The Yukon River Athapaskans and riverine Eskimos of southwestern Alaska preferred traditional traps and deadfalls. They frequently dismantled steel traps which the Russian-American Company attempted to introduce and made other tools from the valuable metal. Log cabins were built at the trading posts and this type of dwelling replaced the traditional house form in good fishing and trapping locations. As noted earlier, wearing European clothing was encouraged so the Indians would not use valuable furs for the purpose. Nevertheless, the practical and highly functional winter footgear, mittens, and caribou skin parkas have continued in use to the present time.

Trapping furbearing animals for trade involved a different kind of settlement pattern than was characteristic of a way of life based on hunting and fishing for direct consumption. In addition to setting a line of traps, the trapper was required to lay in a store of supplies to provide for himself and his family while he was engaged in the arduous and virtually full-time task of setting and checking his traps throughout the season. In making a satisfactory adjustment to this situation, the trapper had to take a number of factors into consideration, including the remoteness of his trapline from the post, the extent to which he desired and was dependent on trade goods, the availability of furbearing animals, and the amount of credit he could secure from the trader. All these factors resulted in decreased mobility. During the stabilized fur trade period, each trading post had its area of influence and virtually all Indians spent at least part of the summer at the posts trading their furs and obtaining credit for the coming season. They then dispersed on winter trapping excursions, frequently leaving their families in permanent dwellings at the post.

The implications of these trends and the introduction of additional factors in more recent times will be discussed in the following chapter. It will be useful, however, to give an illustration of the changes in settlement that occurred in response to changing trading post distribution. Between 1789 when Fort Providence was established at the west end of Great Slave Lake and 1938 when the Hudson's Bay Company opened a post at Uranium City on Lake Athabasca, at least six posts were opened throughout the region. The establishment of each one resulted in a shift in the settlement patterns of various Chipewyan, Dogrib, and Slave bands. The total population of the area became segmented as it was drawn into the spheres of influence of the different posts.

This segmentation can be made clearer by referring specifically to changing settlement patterns at the east end of Great Slave Lake near the close of the stabilized fur trade and mission period. Prior to the establishment of a Hudson's Bay Company post at Snowdrift in 1925, the population of the area consisted of an unknown number of Chipewyan families who hunted, fished, and trapped, moving about the country as single families or as local bands. Most of these people traded periodically at Fort Resolution and considered that community to be their trading and mission center. The Hudson's Bay Company occasionally sent a large canoe loaded with trade items into the country at the east end of the lake. The establishment of the post in 1925 was partly in response to competition from free traders, mobile individuals whose outfits consisted simply of boats loaded with trade items. As in earlier times, these boats intercepted the Indians who were on their way to the post at Fort Resolution and in this manner cut off some of the Company's business. The post at Snowdrift allowed the company to compete more effectively with the free traders, most of whom were eventually driven out of business.

The immediate result of the establishment of a post at Snowdrift was that the Indians hunting and trapping in the area who had previously traded at Fort Resolution now found it convenient to bring their furs to Snowdrift. People who operated within the spheres of influence of other trading centers to the south were also affected. Chipewyan families who normally hunted and trapped in the area between Snowdrift and Lake Athabasca and traded into such centers as Fond-du-Lac, Stony Rapids, Fort Smith, and Fort Fitzgerald, found that it was more convenient for them to trade at the Snowdrift post.

This kind of reorientation of the population was characteristic of much of the Mackenzie drainage and cordilleran region toward the close of the stabilized fur trade and mission period. It does not appear to have occurred in western Alaska where, particularly along the Yukon River and on Cook Inlet, the number of trading posts did not increase markedly following the departure of the Russians. This has probably been due to easier mobility in these areas, to the absence for the most part of competitive free traders, and to the fact that the aboriginal Indians were Central-Based Wanderers rather than Restricted Wanderers. In any event, the tendency for smaller numbers of Indians to be affiliated with a larger number of trading establishments set the stage for the more settled way of life that is characteristic of contemporary Indians throughout northwestern Canada.

Chapter 7

NORTHERN ATHAPASKANS
AND THE MODERN WORLD

In the previous chapter we learned that furs brought the white man into the country of the northern Athapaskan Indians and provided the basis for a relationship between the two peoples for many generations. By the beginning of the twentieth century the entire life style of even the most isolated bands had been modified as a result of what was essentially a business relationship. In the early contact period, most Indians trapped just enough to obtain a few supplies, but later they became increasingly dependent on trade goods, which necessitated an ever greater trapping effort.

The effects of this irreversible development on settlement patterns during the stabilized fur trapping and mission period have been noted. In fact, in no area of Indian life were the changes brought about through a trapping-trading economy more significant than in settlement configurations. These changes greatly facilitated the economic and administrative developments that have occurred throughout the western subarctic in more recent times. For this reason, it is worthwhile to examine more closely the types of trapping-subsistence adaptations that were made throughout the area.

During the early contact period, and in some areas during the stabilized fur trade and mission period as well, Indians tended to gather at the trading posts in tent camps only during the summer months. In winter, families were spread throughout a number of trapping areas, although occasional trips might be made to the post to secure supplies. Later, permanent dwellings, usually constructed of logs, were maintained at the post, but the people continued to be dispersed throughout much of the year and were heavily committed to life in the bush and to the utilization of traditional resources.

A third type of settlement pattern has been characteristic of the Mackenzie River region for several decades. This consists of an all-Indian community occupied by a number of related families from which the men disperse to cover their traplines. Women and children remain in the settlement and the Indians make only brief trips to the trading posts. June Helm (Helm and Leacock, 1971), who has defined and studied this form of settlement, believes that the ecology and terrain of the Mackenzie region encourage this particular adaptation. The river provides easy access to the trading posts even if they are located at some distance, while important lakes in the area provide a year-round supply of fish and their shorelines make good locations for permanent settlements. It is likely that similar easy access to the trading posts in southwestern Alaska resulted in the same kind of settlement pattern in the late nineteenth century, although there is little trace of such settlements at the present time.

A decline in trapping and an increase in government services has brought about a fourth type of settlement pattern characteristic of the modern period. Under these circumstances, families have established permanent, year-round residence at a trading post from which the trappers go out to set and periodically check their traps, returning frequently to the settlement to trade their furs. In this type of settlement, it is also possible for the men to abandon trapping and engage in local subsistence hunting and fishing while depending heavily on various forms of unearned income, particularly welfare subsidies, and occasional wage employment.

THE GOVERNMENT-INDUSTRIAL PERIOD (1940 TO THE PRESENT)

The modern period is characterized by the decline of fur trapping as a major source of income for the Indians, and by the rise of government services, particularly in Canada, along with the emergence of new extractive industries. All of these developments have been extremely important to the Indians and have brought more profound changes in their lives during the past thirty years than occurred in all the earlier contact period. It would be a mistake, however, to overemphasize the decline in trapping. A large proportion of Athapaskans still engage in this activity, though without the vigor of former times. In many communities, it is still the only means by which Indians can earn a cash income, so they are forced to continue trapping even in the face of declining prices and declining satisfaction when measured against their increased knowledge of employment in the outside world. The fact that trapping no longer enables many Indians to fulfill their expectations as consumers does not mean that they are in a position to give it up entirely.

June Helm has placed the beginning of the government-industrial period at about 1940 because, in the preceding year, the value of furs in the Northwest Territories was for the first time less than the value of all other forms of production. It is probable that in Alaska the economic importance of furs began to decline somewhat earlier. At the beginning of World War II, Alaska assumed considerable military importance, bringing with it a great influx of population and the eventual growth of urban centers like Anchorage and Fairbanks within the Athapaskan area. In northwestern Canada, towns like Yellowknife and Fort Smith have grown rapidly and become the seat of governmental as well as industrial activity. It is inevitable that they have exerted considerable influence on the Indians of the region.

A characteristic feature of the extractive industries and dispersed military construction of the modern period has been their operation by imported labor. They have provided only limited employment for Indians who did not in most cases have the education or skills to take advantage of the employment opportunities when they arose. Fishing, small scale lumbering, and some mining and construction work have been exceptions to this general rule, but for the most part, northern commercial activities have been staffed by transient workers from southern Canada and the United States. Indians have only gradually increased their role in northern economic development.

Trapping is, of course, an extractive industry like mining and lumbering, but furbearing animals are only one of the important resources of the western subarctic. Many factors have operated in recent years to make trapping less attractive to northern Athapaskan Indians, but the decline in this activity can be traced primarily to conditions on the world fur market resulting in a marked decline in the prices paid for furs. However, other factors have also been involved in preventing the optimum utilization of the environment for trapping. Some of these will be discussed later in this chapter, but here it can be stated that the combination of an uncomfortable life on the trapline, particularly when compared with settled life in a permanent village, and the unpredictable rewards that often do not seem commensurate with the effort expended, have served to make trapping increasingly unpopular with all Athapaskan Indians.

With the decline in trapping, the trading post has become primarily a commercial store. These posts still buy furs, of course, but their profitable operation depends heavily on the sale of the same kinds of commercial goods that are available in large urban centers. Indians also have access to mail order catalogues and thus, within a relatively few years, have become familiar with virtually the full range of the North American white man's elaborate material culture. An almost total dependence on manufactured goods has been a feature of the government-industrial period. A visitor to an Indian village today will notice such items as outboard motors, stoves, gasoline-operated washing machines, transistor radios, polaroid cameras, sewing machines, chain saws, and many other major items of imported material culture. In addition, many lesser items of everyday use are regularly purchased at the village store. Obviously, low income restricts the Indians' ability to obtain commercial items, but it does not restrict his desire to acquire these goods.

Trapping furbearing animals is a modified-traditional activity, but the decline in trapping has been accompanied throughout the Athapaskan region by a similar decline in the importance of traditional subsistence activities. Again, many factors are involved. Concentration of the population into permanent settlements has meant a less efficient utilization of the environment. Under the new settlement conditions, hunting and trapping are likely to be fairly intensive only in the immediate vicinity of the permanent settlement. Large areas once utilized for the procurement of traditional resources are no longer visited by the Indians or are utilized only occasionally and inefficiently. The growing importance of seasonal wage labor, particularly in Alaska, together with various forms of unearned income, has meant a reduction in the need for and desire to lead the arduous life of a subsistence hunter. In some areas this increasing involvement in a wage economy has made it possible for residents to depend on cash income earned during the summer months, together with a certain amount of subsistence fishing and hunting, to support themselves for the entire year.

Depletion of fur and game resources has also been a major factor in the decline of traditional and modified-traditional subsistence activities in some areas. In the past few years, efficient mechanized snow vehicles have been introduced throughout the western subarctic, abruptly replacing dog teams as a major form of transportation. This has brought about a decline in the importance of subsistence fishing, since families no longer need fish to feed large numbers of dogs. The decline in hunting and fishing has meant a change in diet that has had a significant effect on many Athapaskans: the protein-rich diet of the hunter was much more nutritious than that of the village dweller who depends heavily on store food.

Throughout the Athapaskan area, the federal governments of the United States and Canada have come to play, and indeed to enlarge upon, the role of caretakers to the Indians once filled by the Christian missions. The Canadian government concluded treaties with most of the Indians of eastern Canada in the nineteenth century, but it was not until 1921 that the final treaty was signed with the Indians of the Great Slave Lake area, and that the first representatives of governmental authority, the Royal Canadian Mounted Police (R.C.M.P.), came into the area.

In Alaska, government authority was established somewhat earlier, and although the United States was for a long time reluctant to extend the same rights and privileges to its Athapaskan citizens enjoyed by those in more settled areas to the south, responsibility for educational and medical services had for the most part been taken out of the hands of missionaries long before 1940. The Canadian government, on the other hand, assumed almost no responsibility for such services until after World War II. A few mission hospitals and residential, church-affiliated schools provided the only educational and health facilities available to the Indians of the Canadian Athapaskan area. This situation existed in spite of the fact that under the treaty, Indians were obliged to obey federal laws, presumably in return for government assistance in improving their social, economic, and physical wellbeing.

In Alaska, neither the Indians nor the Eskimos signed treaties with the United States government, nor were they removed from their lands or confined on reservations as their relatives to the south had been. The relatively early advent of government educational and medical services in Alaska can be attributed to the efforts of a few humane, far-seeing individuals and to the fact that toward the close of the nineteenth century, the government assisted various Christian denominations in providing such services. Although this assistance was eventually withdrawn, it served to involve the government in the welfare of Alaskan Indians at a relatively early date.

The legal terms of a government's relations to the Indians under its jurisdiction have, of course, little meaning to the people themselves. To the average Athapaskan of the Great Slave Lake area, Treaty No. 11, under which he is bound to obey the laws of Canada, means little except the modest financial distributions and related entertainments that he associates with the annual Treaty Day. He is aware that the government is a maker of laws, a provider of education, and a dispenser of welfare. In spite of, or perhaps because of, this knowledge, he is likely to view the government as a monolithic and uncontrollable entity, only occasionally subject to manipulation through its local representatives.

In both Alaska and Canada, many Indian families receive a significant percentage of their income from various federal welfare programs. The types of wage labor that have been mentioned are nowhere sufficient to provide steady employment over a long period of time for very many people. The work that does exist is highly seasonal and almost never available locally. In addition, as we have indicated, most Indians are ill-equipped to compete for employment with whites even where jobs exist, since more often than not, their command of English is poor, they lack skills, and they have had little opportunity to acquire practical experience in wage employment situations. Since fur prices are low and the government restricts the number of animals that can be taken, even the present low standard of living characteristic of Athapaskan communities cannot be maintained without additional sources of income. At present, such additional income is available only through government subsidies.

Attempts by Athapaskans in Canada and Alaska to raise their standard of living have been helped in recent decades by certain trends in Indian-government relations throughout North America. In both Canada and the United States there has been a continuing reevaluation of the role of the federal government toward all its citizens, but particularly toward those in minority groups. In both countries the federal governments have established policies which have as their goals the elimination of social, economic, and legal irregularities and the assurance of an acceptable standard of living for all people regardless of where they live. Northern Athapaskans live in remote areas, making it extremely difficult and expensive to provide the kinds of services available in southern urban centers; nevertheless, the right to an acceptable standard of living is meaningful only if it can be achieved in the area where the people have chosen to live. Thus new and expanded welfare programs have been brought to northern peoples, along with the construction of public housing and new medical and educational facilities. At the same time, many of the legal inequalities from which Indians have suffered for many years have been or are in the process of being eliminated.

The effects of these measures are perhaps most noticeable in Canada, where the role of the federal government in the lives of the Indians was minimal before World War II. A most significant advance has been the construction of village schools that enable Athapaskan children to obtain at least a few years of schooling without having to leave home to reside in government boarding schools. Although an important step in the right direction, these schools are not as effective as they might be owing to inappropriate curriculums and the language and cultural barriers separating students and teachers. The same problems have plagued Alaskan village schools, although they are perhaps less severe due to the longer involvement with American schooling. Canada had also provided more comprehensive social welfare measures, providing to all Canadians, Indians and non-Indians alike, family allowances and a comprehensive old age pension program. Especially important is the family allowance, which provides a small monthly payment for each child in a family. This means a great deal in low income areas like the Canadian northwest. The recently inaugurated food stamp program in the United States, which subsidizes the purchase of food for poor families, has had a similar effect in Alaskan villages.

Visitors to Canadian Athapaskan communities in recent years have noted the increasing number of Euro-Canadians who now live in them as a direct result of greater government involvement in the operation of schooling and welfare programs. Agency superintendents, doctors, nurses, fish and game personnel, and policemen are often either resident in the communities or frequent visitors. Most of these individuals receive only short-term appointments in particular settlements, so the Indians have the problem of dealing with a large number of continually changing officials, each of whom may interpret his duties and obligations differently. The Canadian government always provides excellent facilities for its personnel, and the contrast between their way of life and that of the people they serve is often great. In Alaskan villages, the presence of affluent outsiders is less noticeable, although the schools constructed in some communities in recent years appear palatial when compared to other structures in the settlements. Frequently the only permanently resident Euro-Americans are school teachers and religious personnel.

The material gains made by northern Athapaskans in recent years are impressive, but equally impressive is a growing awareness of the problems they all share, regardless of group affiliation, and of their willingness to work together to solve these problems. This heightened awareness also includes a recognition of the similar problems which Eskimos and other Indians face. Indicative of this sense of identity with other native peoples was the establishment in 1967 of the Alaska Federation of Natives, which includes representatives of most of the Eskimo and Indian groups. This organization has begun to operate as an effective political pressure group, making known the point of view and attitudes of Alaskan natives concerning such issues as land claims based on aboriginal territories, education, economic well-being, game regulations, and the importance of preserving native languages and customs. In an era when minority groups have far more strength than they ever had in the past, Indian and Indian-affiliated organizations represent a development of considerable political significance.

In spite of these very real achievements, however, problems are great and pressure for their solution is building. Increased exposure to information concerning the white man's standard of living has raised the level of Indian consumer aspirations considerably. It is becoming abundantly clear that these aspirations cannot be satisfied by their economic base as it now exists. Since the great majority of Athapaskans no longer depend exclusively on the land as a source of subsistence and have lost much of their knowledge of the environment and how to exploit it, they are rapidly approaching a condition in which they are no longer adequately equipped to live in their ancestral territories. Such developments have perhaps made it easier for band and group identity to be submerged in the various Pan-Indian movements that have arisen in Alaska and northwestern Canada. Such organizations as the Alaska Federation of Natives, and groups with more restricted membership like the Union of British Columbia Chiefs, the Copper River Native Association, and the Tanana Chiefs' Conference, have as their goal the exertion of political pressure for the recognition of Indians as a depressed minority within the tantalizingly affluent North American society. It is significant, however, that despite their removal from the traditional manner of exploiting the environment in which they live, the Indians' attachment to their homeland is the strong basis on which all their programs and hopes for the future rest.

CONTEMPORARY INDIAN LIFE—THE VILLAGE OF OLD CROW

In this chapter and the previous one we have seen that the acquisition by northern Athapaskans of European material culture and their increasing involvement in the white man's economy has had an important effect on settlement patterns. The end result of the series of changes under examination has been the establishment of permanent communities throughout those areas formerly occupied by Restricted Wanderers. To further clarify the nature of these developments, and to provide a more detailed picture of a contemporary Canadian Athapaskan community, we will focus on the Kutchin village of Old Crow, located on the Porcupine River, a major tributary of the Yukon. Although situated just inside the Canadian border, Old Crow has been influenced by developments on both sides of the border and at various times in its history has looked both east and west.

The early history of European contact in the eastern Kutchin area parallels that of other regions we have discussed. Trading posts were first established in Kutchin territory, in 1840 at Fort McPherson on the Peel River near its confluence with the Mackenzie and in 1847 at Fort Yukon on the Yukon River. As a result, the traditional seasonal cycle was modified to include summer residence at one or the other of these posts. The cooperative techniques of hunting and fishing characteristic of the aboriginal period were abandoned after the introduction of such individually used items as firearms and commercial fish nets. Increasing dependence on trade goods led the Kutchin, like other Athapaskans, to a greater involvement in the fur trade. Individual trappers became bound to the trading posts through the debt-credit system. Families visited the posts during the summer and at Christmas and Easter holidays, but for much of the year they were dispersed in a series of camps with their associated traplines.

The area around the present settlement of Old Crow near the point where the Crow River joins the Porcupine was the center of activity for the Vunta Kutchin regional band long before the coming of the white man. Fishing is good, and a semiannual caribou migration can be observed from vantage points in the area. During the early contact period, the region served as a gathering place for families from the upper Porcupine who were on their way to trade at Fort Yukon. Permanent dwellings were built as early as 1900, and as the number of inhabitants grew and the length of time spent there increased, the new community began to attract the attention of agents of contact such as traders, missionaries, and the R.C.M.P.

In 1911–1912 a severe smallpox epidemic occurred at Rampart House, where the Hudson's Bay Company had moved from Fort Yukon following the sale of Alaska to the United States. In 1912, two independent traders opened a post at Old Crow and the population shifted there from the disease-ravaged older community. An Anglican church was built in 1926 and two years later the R.C.M.P. moved from Rampart House. The presence of a church, trading post, and police barracks emphasized the importance of the community and people from the surrounding area were attracted to it. More cabins were built and more people, particularly those employed by the agents of contact and those with nearby summer fishing sites, began to live permanently in the community.

The height of the fur trade in the Old Crow area was from the 1920s through the 1950s. At this time, the seasonal cycle included winter and spring trapping and late summer fishing along the Crow and Porcupine rivers. People gathered at Old Crow in the summer and at Christmas and Easter as they had earlier. Some families had cabins in the community, but others lived in tents. Time spent in the community was characterized by heightened social activities. There was gambling, drinking, and courtship, as old ties were renewed and new ones established before people returned to the isolation of their traplines. Physically, Old Crow consisted during this period of a number of log cabins, a log church, an R.C.M.P. barracks, and a trading post. These structures were close together in several rows facing the Porcupine River, and, of course, there were many tents during the periods when people came into the community from their traplines. In addition to the Indian inhabitants, there were also a number of metis, or mixed bloods, white trappers permanently resident in the community, and missionaries and policemen. The Indian dwellings were generally located "uptown" (upriver), while whites and metis lived "downtown."

In the early 1970s, Old Crow looks somewhat different than it did at the height of the fur trade. The settlement pattern reflects the fact that the government has come to play an increasingly large role in the life of the Indians. Beginning in 1961, various government agencies constructed modern facilities in the community. A nursing station and large school were built in that year, and after the school burned in 1969, a new one was constructed in 1970. Here as elsewhere in northern Canada and Alaska, the construction of a school was a major factor responsible for the permanent settlement of families in the community. Those traditionally-oriented families who preferred life away from the village were required to send their children to school, thus reducing their mobility. Once families were forced to remain all year in the community, the activities of even the most mobile family head were severely limited. Maintaining traplines away from the village has virtually ended, although some families still go to muskrat trapping areas in the spring when school is out. In 1961 an anthropologist who visited Old Crow noted that about one-third of the dwellings in the town were tents. In 1968 there were no families occupying tents, all residents having constructed log cabins for year-round living. Fishing has declined along with trapping, and only a few families maintain fish camps. The introduction of snowmobiles to replace dog teams has been at least partly responsible for this significant change.

Subsistence fishing and trapping may have declined, but the people of Old Crow still derive a significant proportion of their diet from hunting and fishing. At the same time, however, they have become increasingly dependent on food purchased from the local store. The Indians are consumer-oriented, spending their money on clothing, capital equipment, liquor, and the many gadgets that are associated with the white man's material culture.

Although the construction of the school may have been central to the ultimate transformation of Old Crow into a permanently settled community, one recent investigator believes that the real rationale for year-round residence in the village is economic. Fur prices have been in steady decline since the 1950s, while the opportunities for wage employment in the village have increased. The school employs four full-time janitors and workers are needed to cut and sell the wood that is used to heat the building. There have been oil explorations in the region in recent years and this activity may eventually bring additional job opportunities to the community. In addition, village men are increasingly willing to leave the settlement to seek seasonal employment. Government assistance, particularly welfare payments and family allowances, have apparently affected Kutchin social organization by reducing the importance of the male in the household. This could be at least a partial explanation for the fact that today 37 percent of Old Crow households are headed by females.

A visitor to Old Crow today would note that the village contains many of the same types of structures that are common to small towns throughout North America. There are the church, the school, and the store, but also a community hall, a nursing station, police facilities, and a baseball diamond. Through programs initiated by the Canadian government, a community freezer has been constructed, new houses built for some families, and electricity made available in all dwellings.

CONCLUSION

Recent investigators in Canadian Athapaskan communities have noted that although changes in settlement patterns have created groupings with the outward appearance of communities, the fact is that traditional definitions of a community seldom apply. People are living together in sizeable numbers and, in most cases, have elected officials who are considered by government agencies to represent the community. In fact, their authority is usually limited to dealings with agency officials and other nonresident whites. Formal community organization almost never operates with regard to strictly local situations. Residents of these communities usually recognize their ties to the community as second to their kinship ties but more important than their ethnic affiliation. Yet community members almost never join in any work for the community as a whole because there are no leaders who can organize activity for the general welfare and improvement of the settlements.

Old Crow is typical of Canadian Athapaskan communities in this respect, but the situation in this settlement is complicated by the presence of a sizeable white population. In the early days of the village, whites were primarily trappers whose way of life did not differ greatly from their Indian neighbors. Today, most are government or church officials who live and work in modern buildings. Thus the gap between their way of life and that of the Indians has become greater. Also, the whites are rotated to other locations frequently and thus do not consider themselves to be members of the community of Old Crow. It appears true, therefore, that the residents of Old Crow and other Canadian Athapaskan settlements occupied by former Restricted Wanderers have not been successful in developing social mechanisms to cope with the problems of living in large, permanent settlements.

In the past, cultural flexibility has been an important Athapaskan adaptive strategy. It is at least possible, therefore, that continuity of location and kinship ties, together with a slowly developing sense of community identity, might eventually create a firm foundation for a formal community organization that would be meaningful in terms of the activities and interests of an entire settlement. Obviously, such an accommodation will be easier in villages that, unlike Old Crow, have a relatively homogeneous population. We have seen that the traditional social organization of Athapaskan bands emphasized the freedom of the individual family and the authority of the family head or the outstanding hunter in a group of families. This individualism is still strongly entrenched in the attitudes of most Athapaskans and will be a decided hindrance in the development of even rudimentary community solidarity. The necessity of developing new forms of leadership and community organization that will keep pace with other aspects of changing culture is of paramount importance.

The grouping of people into permanent settlements has affected kinship and marriage patterns as well as community organization and leadership. Exogamous unilinear kin groups, where they occurred traditionally, have broken down, but modern communities cannot be categorized as either exogamous or endogamous. Propinquity and convenience encourage endogamy, but close consanguinity between many villagers may necessitate the search for a mate outside the community. The bilateral kinship organization of the eastern Athapaskans, because of its flexibility, has been more adaptive than matrilineal organization to the changing circumstances of the historic period.

In the previous chapter we noted that traditional patterns of sharing, although changed somewhat by the introduction of commercial trapping, have retained their importance with reference to important resources in the environment. The emergence of wage labor opportunities might be considered to have put a further strain on aboriginal concepts of sharing, but the importance of individual effort is deeply rooted in traditional Athapaskan culture and may even have been strengthened by recent changes in the economy and settlement patterns.

Although perhaps not affecting sharing patterns to any marked degree, wage labor, welfare payments, and other forms of unearned income have brought about changes in family life and the relationships between family members. As is evident in Old Crow, the payment of a family allowance has reduced the importance of the male in the household, thus loosening the formerly tightly-knit family organization. Wage employment may take men away from their families for long periods of time, and an individual income can mean relative independence for members of an extended family, particularly young, unmarried males. Also, trappers are sometimes more willing to leave their families in the settlement when a predictable income is available to support them. Old age assistance has probably strengthened the position of old people, at least to the extent that they are no longer obliged to accept the charity of their relatives and can maintain their own households.

The residents of Old Crow and other Athapaskan communities have moved in less than fifty years from a way of life based on hunting and fishing to involvement in many of the most basic problems of twentieth century living. An old man who was born in a skin tent and may have paddled a freight canoe for the Hudson's Bay Company or piloted a steamboat transporting prospectors up the Yukon, today learns about the outside world as he listens to his radio. When he becomes ill, a plane arrives at his village to take him to a modern, well-staffed hospital where he can expect to receive expert medical care.

His children, now men in their forties and fifties, were once expert trappers but have either greatly reduced their reliance on income derived from this uncertain activity or have given it up entirely. These men may have had experience as commercial fishermen and lumberjacks or they may be skilled operators of heavy equipment at seasonal construction sites. Almost certainly they have had much fire-fighting experience, often in areas far removed from their native villages. At the very least, these middle-aged men are familiar with items of material culture completely unknown in their fathers' time.

Some of the old man's grandchildren have received elementary education in their community and they may have attended high school in urban centers like Yellowknife, Fort Smith, Fairbanks, Anchorage, and Sitka. The skills acquired at these institutions cannot be used in their native communities and thus they may not return except for periodic visits. At this generational level, the native language has almost completely disappeared in some areas.

Like most Athapaskan villages, Old Crow has an uncertain future. Its economic base is shaky at best and chances for marked improvement are doubtful. The problem is one of securing financial stability for people whose subsistence base no longer provides them with all they need and want, a problem complicated by the unpredictable and therefore demoralizing fluctuations characteristic of a trapping-trading economy. If the people of Old Crow and other communities are to lead useful lives in their traditional environment, and if they are to attain a standard of living comparable to that of people in other rural areas of Canada and the United States, trapping must be replaced by, or at least augmented with, more reliable sources of income.

Obviously, regular wage employment is the answer, but the extractive industries now developing in the north seldom employ large numbers of local people. Since such jobs require special skills, it is simpler and more efficient for the companies involved to import labor from urban centers to the south. Indians are thus likely to face a dilemma in which they must either relocate in an alien environment or accept an artificial existence in their old environment based on massive injections of government subsidies. This is the dilemma already faced by younger, educated Indians, and neither alternative is attractive. Past adaptive mechanisms seem inadequate to provide a solution to such problems. It is little wonder, therefore, that Athapaskans are beginning to search for solutions through a growing activism that seeks to join with other native peoples throughout North America in translating their common social and economic problems into political terms.

Chapter 8

ATHAPASKAN
ADAPTIVE STRATEGY

By way of summary, it will be useful to review briefly the various ways in which an ecologically-oriented analysis has helped us to comprehend the nature of Athapaskan culture and the adaptive processes necessary for survival in a subarctic environment.

In spite of the general uniformity of the northern boreal forest environment, the mountain ranges and major river valleys that are characteristic of northwestern North America have created considerable environmental contrasts in the region occupied by northern Athapaskans. As a result, the various Indian groups have occupied a number of distinct ecological niches, and it is the flexibility of the Athapaskan adaptive framework that has enabled these people to meet the demands of different environments.

Wherever they live, Athapaskans have exploited their total environment. Thus, a certain uniformity has appeared in our consideration of the relationship between the natural environment and subsistence activities. This uniformity is not obscured by the essential distinction we have drawn between upland hunters of big game and the fishermen of river valleys and flats or between Restricted Wandering and Central-Based Wandering forms of settlement patterns. An emphasis on fishing underlies the Central-Based Wandering settlement pattern, but even those groups (such as the Ingalik and Koyukon) who are most dependent on fish also hunt large and small game. In like fashion, upland hunters who are Restricted Wanderers, such as the eastern Kutchin and Upper Tanana, also engage in fishing. In fact, it is probably safe to say that aside from the specialized sea mammal hunting techniques necessary to the coastal dwelling Tanaina, there are very few subsistence methods that are not shared by all Athapaskans.

A comparable uniformity is implicit in many aspects of Athapaskan social organization, and we have attempted to show the close relationship that existed between subsistence techniques and organizational aspects of society. For example, caribou drives as practiced by the Chipewyan and Kutchin required the cooperative efforts of many hunters and, therefore, organization and leadership of a relatively high order. Moose hunting, on the other hand, was most successfully pursued by one or two individuals and leadership roles were largely absent from this activity. On many different levels, Athapaskan social organization could be adjusted to the task at hand, and social institutions generally reflected this ability to meet the demands of the environment at different times of the year and with reference to the organizational requirements of different activities.

The crucial importance of game and knowledge of game animals is graphically demonstrated in the content of Athapaskan mythology and religion. Recognition of a close, kin-like relationship with game animals was in some respects, however, at variance with the importance of hunting and fishing for survival. Since the basic religious relationship was that between an Indian and his animal helper, an individual may have had ambivalent feelings about killing animals for food. It is significant that individual rites were emphasized at the expense of group ceremonies, even among Central-Based Wanderers.

Athapaskans did not form strong social ties beyond the nuclear family and, in fact, reinterpreted a borrowed trait, the potlatch, to the point that it became primarily a rite associated with individual prestige and lacked most of the wider social implications that were characteristic of this ceremony on the northwest coast. Individualism notwithstanding, personal security among these hunters and gatherers was always bolstered by reliable assistance from others in time of need. Thus a bilateral kinship system may be more flexible and more adaptive to the exigencies of life in the western subarctic than a unilineal system because it makes available a greater number of relatives to help the individual when the need arises.

The table on page 124 attempts to summarize selected features of northern Athapaskan adaptive strategy through the association of certain aspects of the traditional culture with the environmental zones into which we have divided the total Athapaskan region. By this time, however, the reader is aware that these zones are not discreet entities and that considerable overlap existed with reference to settlement patterns, subsistence emphasis, and particularly social organization—hence the dotted line divisions in the lower section of the chart.

Those interrelated aspects of social organization shown have been selected because they can be most closely correlated with specific environmental zones. Many aspects of Athapaskan social life (for example band organization, shamanism, and some observances associated with the life cycle) extended across the entire range of environmental zones. Since the same is also true for virtually all subsistence techniques, the significant subsistence emphasis is indicated with subsidiary foci in parentheses. Not reflected in the chart, of course, is that only limited research has been undertaken in some areas with resultant unevenness of known data, or the fact that the cultural groups are unevenly distributed throughout the environmental zones.

Despite these limitations the chart emphasizes the essential cultural homogeneity throughout the area which existed apart from variations in the physical environment, and yet serves to focus attention on the flexibility of the Athapaskan adaptive framework reflected in the evident and significant microadaptations associated with specific environmental zones.

Our examination of the history of European contact in the western subarctic has served to emphasize the importance of geography. The direction of rivers, the presence or absence of lakes and mountain barriers, and proximity to the sea coast have all played major roles in the exposure of northern Athapaskans to outside influences. The fact that Europeans were dependent upon the Indians to harvest furs, virtually the only resource recognized as having economic value throughout much of the contact period, has been the major factor in shaping postcontact

Table 2. Summary of selected features of Northern Athapaskan adaptive strategy

	Arctic drainage lowlands	Cordilleran	Yukon and Kuskokwim River Basins	Cook-Inlet-Susitna River Basin	Copper River Basin
GEOGRAPHIC REGIONS	riverine-lacustrine lowlands	deeply dissected mountains, river valleys	riverine lowlands	coastal lowlands, mountains	rugged mountains
SUBSISTENCE FOCUS AND SETTLEMENT PATTERN	large game hunting (fishing)	large game hunting (fishing in some areas)	fishing (hunting)	sea mammal, large land animal hunting (fishing)	fishing (hunting)
	Restricted Wanderers	Restricted Wanderers (mostly)	Central-Based Wanderers	Central-Based Wanderers	Restricted Wanderers
ASPECTS OF SOCIAL ORGANIZATION	bilateral descent — — — ↑	(hereditary leadership) matrilineal sibs — — ↑ bilateral descent — — ↑	bilateral descent — — ↑ group ceremonies — ↕	(hereditary leadership) matrilineal sibs group ceremonies	matrilineal sibs ↑
	(flexible residence) — — ↓	matrilocal residence — — ↑ (flexible residence)	(flexible residence) — ↑	matrilocal residence	matrilocal residence
		potlatch	potlatch	potlatch	potlatch
		modified vision quest for boys		modified vision quest for boys	
	abandonment of aged	abandonment of aged			abandonment of aged

124

history. The absence until recently of extractive economic activities requiring non-Indian technology and personnel has meant that the location of trading posts, largely determined by geographical factors, was the prime influence on changing Indian subsistence and settlement patterns.

This brief discussion has stressed the importance of cultural flexibility as an Athapaskan adaptive strategy, and it is essential to examine this significant characteristic in more detail. Indians moving into different environments in most cases readily borrowed techniques and technologies from the people already present and accommodated these techniques within Athapaskan culture. Traditional Athapaskan culture must be thought of as essentially an accommodating culture, and accommodation, in turn, greatly facilitated survival in a demanding environment.

In stressing flexibility and accommodation, however, we should not lose sight of a simple and very basic truth that applies to all areas where hunting peoples have exploited their environment: the expert hunter's most important attributes have always been knowledge and intelligence, both highly individual matters. The more a man knew about his environment and the multitude of exploitative techniques that were part of his cultural heritage, the better equipped he was to deal with the environment effectively. Specialized knowledge is in itself an adaptive strategy, and it is indicative of the versatility of northern Athapaskans that they have been able to adjust satisfactorily to a number of environmental circumstances by accepting strong cultural influences from neighboring peoples.

Given the diversity of cultural borrowing and reworking, we may ask whether in fact there is justification for a book on northern Athapaskans. Do these people actually share a distinctive culture pattern, or is "northern Athapaskan" simply a convenient term to refer to an aggregate of geographic and linguistic groupings? The opinion of most specialists agrees with the emphasis in this book; that there are deep cultural similarities among all northern Athapaskan speakers. Specific culture traits may be shared with other peoples, but the reworking of these traits into distinctive culture patterns characterized by a high degree of flexibility and adaptability are not found in their entirety among any other people. These patterns delineate Athapaskan culture as a recognizable entity.

Our ecological approach to the study of northern Athapaskan culture has perhaps raised as many questions as it has answered, but it has at least taken us considerably beyond a consideration of these people as simply a linguistic and geographical grouping. It is an approach that has led Athapaskan specialists to build up the substantive base that should make it possible for later investigators to ask and perhaps eventually answer more sophisticated anthropological questions about the people of the area. This will only be possible, however, through a careful analysis of the complex interplay between environmental, sociocultural, psychological, and historical factors throughout the western subarctic.

Appendix

THE ETHNOGRAPHIC
LITERATURE AND FUTURE
RESEARCH NEEDS

Although a great deal has been written about northern Athapaskan Indians by anthropologists and others, these source materials are neither as balanced nor as complete as one might wish. Athapaskans are, on the whole, better known than their neighbors to the west, the Alaskan Eskimos, although perhaps not so well known anthropologically as the Algonkian-speaking peoples to the east. A brief examination and evaluation of Athapaskan source materials may help to place in perspective the data presented in this book, and serve as an introduction to a consideration of future research needs.

Although I have said very little about the accounts of early exploration in interior Alaska and northwest Canada, a considerable amount of useful ethnographic information concerning northern Athapaskans is to be found in the published writings of the explorers, traders, and missionaries who contacted them between 1700 and 1900. In fact, what little information we have on the precontact way of life of many groups has been derived solely from these historical sources. For example, much of what we know concerning the traditional culture of the Atna comes from Henry T. Allen's (1887) explorations along the Copper River and its tributaries in 1885, while extremely valuable and surprisingly detailed data on the Chipewyan around the time of first contact with Europeans can be found in Samuel Hearne's (1958) account of his explorations, beginning at Fort Churchill and extending to the mouth of the Coppermine River between 1769 and 1772. With a few notable exceptions, however, the ethnographic material in historical accounts is likely to be sparse and uneven at best, and only the most painstaking research involving the comparative use of many documents, both published and archival, enables the ethnohistorian to understand the cultural and societal consequences of Indian-white contact, let alone the nature of the aboriginal culture.

Our knowledge of aboriginal Athapaskan lifeways is limited in spite of the fact that a number of groups were studied during a period when informants could reasonably be expected to recall a time of minimal outside influence. Research by experienced ethnologists began in the early 1900s when Robert Lowie visited the Chipewyan and when G. T. Emmons (1911) and James Teit studied the Tahltan and neighboring groups. A decade later, J. Alden Mason did field work among the Dogrib, while Kai Birket-Smith (1930) paid a brief visit to the eastern Chipewyan, and Pliny Earle Goddard (1916) studied the Beaver. None of these scholars, all of whom are better known for their work among peoples other than Athapaskans, produced detailed ethnographic accounts, and in some cases their studies amount to little more than random ethnographic notes. Some early investigators apparently found Athapaskans difficult to work with and all doubtless suffered from an inability to communicate with the Indians directly; at that time, very little English was spoken by any of the groups.

Intensive studies of northern Athapaskans began in the 1920s. The work of Diamond Jenness among the southern cordilleran peoples reflected the expanding interests of Canadian ethnology, which reached the Pacific during this decade. In a ten-year period, Jenness produced monographs on the Sekani and Sarsi and gathered data on other groups for his monumental *Indians of Canada*, first published in 1932. In 1928 Cornelius Osgood began his extensive research among northern Athapaskans with field work in the Great Bear Lake area. Later he concentrated his efforts in western Alaska, producing detailed monographs on the Kutchin (1936a), Tanaina (1937), and particularly on the Ingalik (1940, 1958, 1959). Robert McKennan's work with the

Upper Tanana (1959) and Chandalar Kutchin (1965) also belongs to this period, although the results of his studies were not published until much later. Also in the 1930s, Robert Sullivan (1942) carried out a detailed study of Koyukon subsistence activities.

Comparable to Osgood's work among Alaskan and Mackenzie drainage Athapaskans is the research of John Honigmann among arctic drainage lowlands and cordilleran peoples. Beginning in 1943, he carried out extensive research, first among the Slave Indians at Fort Nelson (1946), and later with the Kaska (1949, 1954). Although his studies have provided us with much valuable data concerning the traditional cultures of these people, his interests centered on aspects of culture change and he was the first ethnographer to focus on the acculturation of northern Athapaskans. His research was also much more psychologically oriented than the work of anyone else up to that time.

These few individuals produced all the major research on northern Athapaskans prior to World War II. Nevertheless, it resulted in definitive monographs on seven groups, along with considerable information on neighboring peoples. The significance of this accomplishment may be more apparent when it is realized that at a comparable time, there was only one reasonably complete Alaskan Eskimo ethnography.

Following the war, a younger generation of anthropologists began to work in the Athapaskan area and their number has proliferated to the point where a recent listing of scholars with Athapaskan research interests in linguistics, archaeology, and ethnography contains more than ninety names. Much of this research is very recent and, for the most part, unpublished. Without going into detail, it is possible to note certain trends in contemporary Athapaskan research indicating the direction in which it is moving, but also showing that although much work has been done, there are still extensive gaps. The fact is that in spite of the intensity of recent research, there are still some areas about which virtually nothing is known and others where our knowledge has not been increased since the work of the pioneer ethnologists in the 1920s and 1930s.

Most Athapaskan research in recent years has involved Canadian groups, particularly those in the arctic drainage lowlands. This focus is at least partly fortuitous, but has been influenced to some extent by the availability of Canadian government support for research in the Northwest Territories and contract grants from the National Museum of Canada. Thus in the past fifteen years, studies have been made of Chipewyan, Dogrib, Slave, Hare, and Kutchin communities. The major thrust of most of these studies has been ecological, the authors concentrating on ways in which human life has been shaped by factors in the external environment. The emphasis in most of these studies is on social organization, reflecting particular concern with the band organization of hunting and gathering peoples which is itself related to the current interest in ecologically-oriented studies. Another emphasis has been on problems of culture change and government administration. Scholars have certainly not neglected historical data, but there have been only a few attempts to reconstruct the aboriginal way of life of the peoples in question. Such reconstructions would be difficult at best, and there is no doubt that in a few years they will be impossible.

In addition to the recent studies just mentioned, specialists have also worked among the Atna in Alaska and the Tutchone and related peoples in the southern cordilleran area. These studies, not yet published, will have a more traditional focus and presumably a stronger historical emphasis. They are important since they will provide us with information concerning several of the least known Athapaskan groups.

With the exception of that on the Atna, research on Athapaskans in Alaska in recent years has been very limited and this fact is reflected in the preceding pages, particularly in chapter 7. There is only one published study of a modern Alaskan Athapaskan community; an ecological analysis of a western Kutchin village. Much of the work that has been done has a strong historical emphasis: the research carried out among the Tanaina and Ingalik is primarily concerned with the effects of Russian and American contact with the Indians in the nineteenth century. It is somewhat surprising that the most western Athapaskan groups have not attracted more interest on the part of ethnologists and students of culture change, particularly since good base-line ethnographies exist for some of the groups in this area. It is likely, however, that the continuing interest in human ecology, which has encouraged a kind of renaissance in the study of hunting and gathering peoples, will eventually result in greater and more varied research in this area. For the moment, however, the northwestern Athapaskans of Alaska continue to be neglected by younger specialists. In a recent issue of *The Western Canadian Journal of Anthropology* (Vol. 2, No. 1, 1970) devoted to Athapaskan studies, only two articles out of a total of thirteen concern Pacific drainage peoples, and both papers have a strong historical rather than ecological emphasis.

Although the linguistic unity of northern Athapaskans has long been recognized, the only ethnographer to concern himself with all the groups has been Cornelius Osgood. He concentrated his efforts on determining the maximal societal-dialectic groups and their areas of resource utilization, but he did not attempt an integrative study of northern Athapaskans, and no later student had ventured such a general overview. One explanation of this lack of an integrative approach can be found in the environmental setting, which, as Osgood first noted, separates Athapaskans into two major groupings, those of the arctic and Pacific drainages.

The physiographic division is a real one and perhaps has had a greater influence on the attitudes and approaches of ethnologists than they themselves would generally recognize. Specialists who have studied arctic drainage peoples tend to look east for cultural influences in both the protocontact and contact periods, while those who have studied the western groups in the Pacific drainage naturally concern themselves with cultural influences, both aboriginal and postcontact, that came from the west. Since no specialist other than Osgood has worked with groups in both areas, few have attempted to see the region as a whole. In fact, some have questioned whether the unit actually exists, a problem that we discussed in chapter 8. In any event, the nature of contacts of the last 250 years together with the precontact conditions of physical and cultural environment are such that researchers with eastern interests and experience have felt that the information they obtained from their studies was more comparable to that obtained on peoples further to the east than what was known of peoples to the west. These differences are perhaps more apparent than real, and even the historical factors operating to influence the culture of Indians in the arctic and Pacific drainages are part of a tradition of contact that has wide applications throughout North America.

Readers will have noted that my discussion of northern Athapaskan lifeways has been more extensive than intensive. In part, of course, this reflects the breadth of the subject area and the introductory nature of this book, but it is also the result of the real gaps in the literature that are apparent from our brief review of the published writings of Athapaskan specialists. We will discuss here some of the more obvious gaps in our knowledge that need to be filled. Time is of the utmost importance. It is too late to secure complete ethnographies, truly definitive information concerning precontact lifeways being already beyond our reach. Nevertheless, some data on selected aspects of the aboriginal culture can still be collected and, of course, contemporary people and problems can be studied. By refining our concepts and our methods, we can bring more sophisticated interpretations to bear on the restricted amounts of information that are still available.

Even though much recent research has emphasized social organization, it is clear that more details are badly needed for many of the groups. Although complete reconstruction may be impossible, some information can still be obtained from older informants. Our difficulties in defining bands and in assessing the significance of unilinear descent groups attest to the need for this kind of information. Likewise, we have been unable to say anything definite about either the antiquity of matriliny among northwestern Athapaskans, or the role of the tripartite sib system.

Basic ethnographic data for many of the Athapaskan groups is lacking. The Koyukon are perhaps the least known, but the culture of some of the southern cordilleran groups is also far from completely understood, and researchers will have to rely heavily on ethnohistoric sources to supplement data from older informants. Some of the more obvious gaps in the ethnographic record, particularly with reference to the Atna and some of the southern cordilleran groups, will be filled with the publication of recently-completed research.

Recent work in the long-neglected field of Athapaskan prehistory is doing much to fill gaps in our knowledge of cultural developments in northwestern North America. Particularly useful would be additional information concerning the late prehistoric and protohistoric periods. Population size and general settlement configuration during the eighteenth and nineteenth centuries for sites that can definitely be identified with existing cultural-dialectic groups would provide information to augment the limited ethnographic data that can now be collected. Perhaps here more than in some other regions of North America, the data provided by archeology can be successfully combined with that of ethnography to give depth to the study of culture change in an area where outside influences were considerable and knowledge of the ethnographic past is extremely limited.

Earlier we discussed some of the factors that set the culture of the northwestern Athapaskans apart from that of arctic drainage peoples and noted that many of these distinctive traits were related to a dependence on salmon. If this is too simple an explanation of the differences between the two regions, a good deal more research is needed to understand the nature of the truly distinctive features. It seems likely that the cultures of the Alaskan interior may provide the most significant information concerning these distinctions.

Similarly, a more sophisticated understanding of the many elements common to the cultures of the northwest coast and the western Athapaskans is necessary. The usual explanation of diffusion is too simplistic and fails to take into consideration the considerable historical depth of some of these traits within the Athapaskan area.

At this late date, community studies are about all that we can use to get detailed information concerning social process, and, as previously noted, a number of such studies have been made in the Mackenzie drainage. Such research is lacking, however, for the peoples of interior and western Alaska, and it is particularly unfortunate that there is no study of a contemporary community of Central-Based Wanderers. We are thus without data for comparison with the information available on the adaptive mechanisms developed by former Restricted Wanderers of the Mackenzie drainage for their dealings with the problems of the contemporary world.

Finally, a much more detailed understanding of the nature of Athapaskan languages is needed, particularly relating to the significance of the many regional dialects. Such studies are in progress, but as yet little information of use to the ethnographer has been published.

Selected References

This listing is restricted to those articles and monographs utilized extensively in the preceding pages. Following these references is an annotated list of suggested further reading on all aspects of northern Athapaskan life, past and present. These sources were also consulted during the preparation of this book.

BEARDSLEY, R. K. et al.
>   1956 "Functional and evolutionary implications of community patterning." R. Wauchope, ed., *Seminars in Archaeology: 1955.* Society for American Archaeology, Memoir 11: 129–157.

COHEN, R. AND J. W. VANSTONE
>   1963 "Dependency and self-sufficiency in Chipewyan stories." National Museum of Canada, bulletin 194: 29–55.

DARNELL, R., Ed.
>   1970 Special Issue: Athabascan studies. *Western Canadian Journal of Anthropology,* vol. 2, no. 1 (whole issue).

HELM, J.
>   1961 *The Lynx Point People: The dynamics of a northern Athapaskan band.* Ottawa, National Museum of Canada, bulletin 176.
>   1965 "Bilaterality in the socio-territorial organization of the arctic drainage Dene." *Ethnology* 4: 361–385.
>   1968 "The nature of Dogrib socioterritorial groups." R. B. Lee and I. DeVore, Eds., *Man the hunter,* pp. 118–125. Chicago, Aldine.

HELM, J. AND E. B. LEACOCK
  1971 "The hunting tribes of subarctic Canada." E. B. Leacock and N. O. Lurie, Eds., *North American Indians in historical perspective*, pp. 343–374. New York, Random House.
HELM, J. et al.
  "The contact history of the subarctic Athapaskans." Ottawa, National Museum of Man (in press).
HONIGMANN, J. J.
  1946 *Ethnography and acculturation of the Fort Nelson Slave.* New Haven, Yale University Publications in Anthropology, no. 33.
  1949 *Culture and ethos of Kaska society.* New Haven, Yale University Publications in Anthropology, no. 40.
JENNESS, D.
  1958 *The Indians of Canada.* Ottawa, National Museum of Canada. First published 1932 as Bulletin 65 in Anthropological Series No. 15.
McCLELLAN, C.
  1964 "Culture contacts in the early historic period in northwestern North America." *Arctic Anthropology* 2: 3–15.
  1970 "Introduction." Special issue: Athabascan studies, *Western Canadian Journal of Anthropology* 2: vi–xix.
McKENNAN, R. A.
  1959 *The Upper Tanana Indians.* New Haven, Yale University Publications in Anthropology, no. 55.
  1965 *The Chandalar Kutchin.* Montreal, Arctic Institute of North America, technical paper no. 17.
  1969 "Athapaskan groupings and social organization in central Alaska." Ottawa, National Museum of Canada, bulletin 228, pp. 93–115.
OSGOOD, C. B.
  1933 "The ethnography of the Great Bear Lake Indians." Ottawa, National Museum of Canada, Annual Report, 1931, pp. 31–97.
  1936a *Contributions to the ethnography of the Kutchin.* New Haven, Yale University Publications in Anthropology, no. 14.
  1936b *The distribution of northern Athapaskan Indians.* New Haven, Yale University Publications in Anthropology, no. 7.
  1937 *The ethnography of the Tanaina.* New Haven, Yale University Publications in Anthropology, no. 16.

1940 *Ingalik material culture.* New Haven, Yale University Publications in Anthropology, no. 22.

1958 *Ingalik social culture.* New Haven, Yale University Publications in Anthropology, no. 53.

1959 *Ingalik mental culture.* New Haven, Yale University Publications in Anthropology, no. 56.

SLOBODIN, R.

1962 *Band organization of the Peel River Kutchin.* Ottawa, National Museum of Canada, bulletin 179.

VANSTONE, J. W.

1963 "Changing patterns of Indian trapping in the Canadian subarctic." *Arctic* 16: 159–174.

1965 *The changing culture of the Snowdrift Chipewyan.* Ottawa, National Museum of Canada, bulletin 209.

WELSH, A.

1970 "Community pattern and settlement pattern in the development of Old Crow Village, Yukon Territory." *Western Canadian Journal of Anthropology* 2: 17–30.

Suggested Further Reading

ALLEN, H. T.

1887 *Report on an expedition to the Copper, Tanana, and Koyu-kon rivers, in the Territory of Alaska, in the year 1885. . . .* Washington, U.S. Government Printing Office. [An important travel account that includes the first description of the Atna.]

BIRKET-SMITH, K.

1930 *Contributions to Chipewyan ethnology.* Copenhagen, Report of the Fifth Thule Expedition, 1921–24, vol. VI, no. 3. [An early study that emphasizes material culture and mythology.]

DUMOND, D. E.

1969 "Toward a prehistory of the Na-Dene, with a general comment on population movements among nomadic hunters." *American Anthropologist* 71: 857–863. [Stimulating speculations concerning Athapaskan prehistory.]

EMMONS, G. T.

1911 *The Tahltan Indians* Philadelphia, University of Pennsylvania, the Museum, Anthropological Publication, vol. IV, no. 1. [The basic ethnographic study of these southern cordilleran peoples.]

GILLESPIE, B. C.

1970 "Yellowknives: quo iverunt?" Proceedings of the 1970 Annual Spring Meeting, American Ethnological Society, pp. 61–71. [An evaluation of historical data on the now-extinct Yellowknife Indians.]

GODDARD, P. E.

1916 *The Beaver Indians.* Anthropological Papers of the American Museum of Natural History, vol. X, pt. IV. [A basic ethnography with emphasis on material culture and folklore.]

HALL, E. S.

    1969 "Speculations on the late prehistory of the Kutchin Athapaskans." *Ethnohistory* 16: 317–333. [Oral historical, archeological, ecological, linguistic, and ethnological data is utilized to delineate Kutchin boundaries in late prehistoric times.]

HEARNE, S.

    1958 *A journey from Prince of Wales Fort in Hudson's Bay to the Northern Ocean in the years 1769, 1770, 1771, 1772.* Richard Glover, Ed. Toronto, Macmillan. [Hearne traveled extensively with the Chipewyan and described their early contact way of life in considerable detail.]

HELM, J.

    1965 "Patterns of allocation among the Arctic drainage Dene." Proceedings of the 1965 Annual Spring Meeting, American Ethnological Society, pp. 33–45. [On the allocation of natural resources among Athapaskans of the upper Mackenzie.]

    1972 "The Dogrib Indians." G. G. Bicchieri, Ed., Hunters and gatherers today, pp. 51–83. New York, Holt, Rinehart and Winston. [A concise summary of Dogrib ethnography and culture change.]

HELM, J. AND N. O. LURIE

    1961 The subsistence economy of the Dogrib Indians of Lac La Martre in the Mackenzie District of the Northwest Territories. Ottawa, Northern Coordination and Research Centre, Department of Northern Affairs and National Resources. [An excellent, detailed study of contemporary Dogrib subsistence.]

HOIJER, H.

    1963 "The Athapaskan languages." Studies in the Athapaskan languages, University of California Publications in Linguistics 29: 1–29. [An authoritative paper on modern Athapaskan linguistic structures.]

HONIGMANN, J. J.

    1954 *The Kaska Indians: an ethnographic reconstruction.* New Haven, Yale University Publications in Anthropology, no. 51. [A detailed study of pre-contact Kaska ethnography.]

JENNESS, D.

    1937 *The Sekani Indians of British Columbia.* Ottawa, National Museum of Canada, bulletin 84. [An early ethnography with emphasis on religion and ritual.]

    1938 *The Sarcee Indians of Alberta.* Ottawa, National Museum of Canada, bulletin 90. [A brief but well-rounded ethnography based on field work in the early 1920s.]

KRAUSE, M. E.
1964 Review of "Studies in the Athapaskan languages" (Hoijer).
International Journal of American Linguistics 30: 409–415.
[A comprehensive analysis of recent studies on the structure of Athapaskan languages.]

MACNEISH, J. H. (JUNE HELM)
1956 "Leadership among northeastern Athabascans." *Anthropologica* 2: 131–163. [A survey of Mackenzie drainage Athapaskan socio-political organization based primarily on historic sources.]

MCKENNAN, R. A.
1969 "Athapaskan groups of central Alaska at the time of white contact." *Ethnohistory* 16: 335–343. [The impact of white contact and recent linguistic data are evaluated in an effort to generalize about aboriginal Athapaskan economies and territorial boundaries.]

MORLAN, R. E., Ed.
1970 "Symposium on northern Athabascan prehistory." Canadian Archaeological Association, bulletin no. 2, pp. 1–43. [A collection of five papers on recent archaeological research in the Athapaskan region.]

NELSON, R. K.
1973 *Hunters of the northern forest. Designs for survival among the Alaskan Kutchin.* Chicago, University of Chicago Press. [Subsistence ecology of contemporary Kutchin in the Yukon Flats area.]

OSGOOD, C. B.
1971 *The Han Indians: A compilation of ethnographic and historical data on the Alaska-Yukon boundary area.* New Haven, Yale University Publications in Anthropology, no. 74. [The only study of this nearly extinct group.]

SLOBODIN, R.
1960 "Eastern Kutchin warfare." *Anthropologica*, n.s., 2: 76–93. [On the relations between eastern Kutchin bands and their Indian and Eskimo neighbors.]

SULLIVAN, R. J.
1942 *The Ten'a food quest.* Washington, D.C., the Catholic University of America, Anthropological Series, no. 11. [On the seasonal subsistence cycle of the Koyukon Indians.]

WEST, F. H.
1959 "On the distribution and territories of the western Kutchin tribes." Anthropological Papers of the University of Alaska 7: 113–116. [New evidence concerning the northern and western boundaries of Kutchin territory.]

Index

Abandonment of the aged
  Chipewyan, 83
  Kaska, 83
  Sekani, 83
  Slave, 83
Adaptation
  flexibility and, 2, 3, 4, 5, 6, 9, 23, 24,
      30, 31, 32, 117, 118, 120, 121,
      122, 123, 124, 125
Afterlife
  attitudes toward, 63
Aggression, 95, 96
Alaska Federation of Natives, 112, 113
Allen, H. T., 127
Amulets, 64
Animal power, 65, 66
  Bear Lake Indians, 65
  Dogrib, 65
Archaeology, 4, 5
Athapaskan Indians
  boundaries with Eskimos, 18, 19
  distribution of, 8, 9, 10, 14, 15, 17, 18,
      20, 43
  influence of neighbors on, 5, 6, 23, 60
  integrative studies of, 131
  movements of people, 39, 40
  political affiliations, 112, 113
  recent research on, 129, 130–133
Atna
  distribution of, 20
  dwellings, 33, 37
  fur trade, 95
  matrilineal sib organization, 52
  potlatch, 56
  subsistence, 30, 31

Band organization, 54, 57, 58
  Ingalik, 44
  Koyukon, 44
Barren Grounds, 35
Bear Lake Indians
  animal power, 65
  dwellings, 34, 35
  infanticide, 76
  revitalization movements, 71, 72

Beardsley, R. K., 37, 38
Beaver Indians
  distribution of, 15
  fur trade, 95
  European contact, 15
Birket-Smith, K., 128
Boundaries
  Athapaskan-Eskimo, 18, 19
Bride service, 81, 82

Canadian government
  services of, 107, 109–112
  treaties, 109, 110
Cannibalism, 27
Carrier
  disposal of dead, 85
  influenced by plateau, 17
  leadership, 49
  matrilineal sib organization, 52
  potlatch, 56
  puberty rites, boys, 80
Ceremonies
  Ingalik, 70
  Tahltan, 70
Chandalar Kutchin
  leadership, 48
  life cycle, 84–85, 87
  old age, 83
  missionaries and, 99
  mythology, 60
  revitalization movements, 72
  shamanism, 67, 68
  subsistence, 26, 27
  warfare, 48, 49, 50
Chilcotin
  influenced by plateau, 17
  leadership, 49
Childbirth, 77
  Ingalik, 77
  Kutchin, 77
  Upper Tanana, 77
"Chinook," 14
Chipewyan
  abandonment of the aged, 83
  distribution of, 14, 15

Chipewyan (cont'd)
  dwellings, 35
  European contact, 14
  fur trade, 92, 93, 95, 103, 104
  infancy, 78
  leadership, 48
  old age, 82–83
  subsistence, 24, 25, 26
  warfare, 50
Cook, J., 94
Cough Child, 71
Cremation, 84–85

Dead, disposal of, 84–85
  Carrier, 85
  Chandalar Kutchin, 85
  Ingalik, 85
  Kaska, 85
  Kutchin, 85
  Sekani, 85
  Slave, 85
  Tahltan, 85
  Tanaina, 85
  Upper Tanana, 85
Death, 83, 84
  Chandalar Kutchin, 84
  Slave, 83
  Tanaina, 84
  Upper Tanana, 83, 84
Descent, bilateral, 53
  Ingalik, 52
  Koyukon, 52
Descent groups, 58
Division of labor, 78–79
Divorce, 82
Dixon, G., 94
Dogrib
  animal power, 65
  distribution of, 14, 15
  fur trade, 92
  leadership, 48
  social groupings, 45–47
Dwellings, 32
  Atna, 33, 37
  Bear Lake Indians, 34, 35
  Chipewyan, 35
  Ingalik, 35, 36
  Kutchin, 33, 34
  Slave, 35
  Tanaina, 36, 37
  Upper Tanana, 33, 34, 37

Emmons, G. T., 128
Employment. See Wage employment.
Epidemics, 57, 93, 96, 114
Eskimos, 1, 3, 4, 53, 88, 92
  boundaries with Athapaskans, 18, 19
  influence on Athapaskans 6, 17, 20, 23,
    29, 30, 35, 36, 42, 60, 67, 70
  subsistence, 31
  trade with Europeans, 94
  war with Athapaskans, 50
European contact, 90
  alcohol, 93
  economic activities, 91–94, 97–98, 107–
    108, 119–120
  effects on social organization, 44, 47, 52
  epidemics, 93, 96, 114

influence on traditional religious beliefs,
    73
  inter-Indian aggression and, 95
  resource utilization and, 108
  Russians and Athapaskans, 93, 95, 96
  settlement patterns and, 95, 112–118
Exploration, 127, 128

Fish wheel, 28, 29
Flora and fauna
  changing distribution of, 20, 21, 22
  native traditions about, 21, 22
Food scarcity, 31
Frontiers, types of, 100, 101
Fur trade, 91
  contrasted with mining and homestead-
    ing, 100
  decline of, 106, 107, 108–109, 120
  early contact period, 92, 93
  Indian adaptation to, 101–104
  Indians
    Atna, 95
    Beaver, 95
    Chipewyan, 92, 94, 95, 103, 104
    Dogrib, 92
    Han, 98
    Ingalik, 94
    Koyukon, 94, 95
    Kutchin, 98
    Peel River Kutchin, 41
    Tahltan, 98
    Tanaina, 29, 94, 95, 98
    Tutchone, 98
    Upper Tanana, 98
    Yellowknife, 92, 95
  missionaries and, 100
  network of trading posts, 96
  northwest coast and Athapaskans, 98
  settlement patterns and, 103–106, 108
  trading monopolies, 97

Game, beliefs about
  Tanaina, 21
  Upper Tanana, 21
Ghost dance, 71
Goddard, P. E., 128

Han
  fur trade, 98
  potlatch, 56
Hearne, S., 92, 93, 128
Helm, J., 45, 54, 100, 106, 107
Homesteading, 100
Honigmann, J. J., 129
Hudson's Bay Co., 21, 92, 93, 98, 99, 103,
    114, 119

Individualism, 59, 60, 101, 118
Infancy, 77–78
  Chipewyan, 78
  Bear Lake Indians, 76
  Ingalik, 76
Infanticide, 76
Ingalik
  band organization, 44
  bilateral descent, 52
  ceremonies, 70
  childbirth, 77

disposal of dead, 85
distribution of, 9, 18
dwellings, 35, 36
fur trade, 94
potlatch, 56
preferential marriage, 81
settlement patterns, 41, 42
social groupings, 45, 47
subsistence, 28, 29
Insects, 18

Jenness, D., 128
Juvenal, Father, 98

Kashim, 36, 42, 70, 85
Kaska
abandonment of the aged, 83
bride service, 81
disposal of the dead, 85
matrilineal sib organization. 52
mythology, 62
personality, 88–89
polyandry, 81
preferential marriage, 81
puberty rites, boys, 79
shamanism, 66
Koyukon
band organization, 44
bilateral descent, 52
distribution of, 9, 17, 18
fur trade, 94, 95
potlatch, 56
settlement patterns, 42
Kutchin
childbirth, 77
disposal of the dead, 85
dwellings, 33, 34
fur trade, 98
matrilineal sib organization, 52
matrilocal residence, 53
potlatch, 56
teknonomy, 78

Levirate, 53
Leadership
Carrier, 49
Chandalar Kutchin, 48
Chilcotin, 49
Chipewyan, 48
Dogrib, 48
Slave, 48
Tahltan, 49
Tanana, 49
Upper Tanana, 49
Life cycle, 74–76, 85–86
Chandalar Kutchin, 87
Snowdrift Chipewyan, 86
Upper Tanana, 87
Lowie, R., 128

McClellan, C., 9
McKennan, R. A., 72, 128
Mackenzie Eskimos, 41
Mason, J. A., 128
Matrilineal sib organization, 49, 51, 52, 53
Atna, 52
Carrier, 52
Kaska, 52

Kutchin, 52
Tagish, 52
Tahltan, 52
Tanaina, 52
Tanana, 52
Tutchone, 52
Matrilocal residence, 53, 82
Menopause, 82
Mining, 100
Missionary activity
fur trade and, 100
Hudson's Bay Co. and, 99
medical services and, 109
Protestant and Roman Catholic, 98, 99
Russian Orthodox Church, 98, 99
schools, 99, 109
Mythology, 60, 61, 62, 63
Chandalar Kutchin, 60
Kaska, 62
Upper Tanana, 61

Na-Dene speech family. 4. 5
Nakhani, 63. 64
Naming, 78
Northwest Coast
influence on Athapaskans, 6, 17, 52,
55–56, 60, 70, 85, 94, 96
Northwest Co., 93

Old age, 82, 87
Old Crow, 113–120
Orphans, 78
Osgood, C., 62, 72, 128

Peel River Kutchin
fur trade, 41
settlement patterns, 41
warfare, 50
Personality, 88–89
Physical environment, 9, 11–13, 15–21
Polyandry, 53, 81
Polygyny, 53, 81
Pond, P., 92, 93
Population, 11
Portlock, Capt. N., 94
Potlatch, 49, 55, 56, 57
Atna, 56
Carrier, 56
Han, 56
Ingalik, 56
Koyukon, 56
Kutchin, 56
Tahltan, 56
Tanana, 56
Upper Tanana, 55, 56
Preferential marriage
Ingalik, 81
Kaska, 81
Slave, 80, 81
Tanaina, 81
Upper Tanana, 81
Pregnancy, 76, 77
Puberty rites, boys, 79, 80
Puberty rites, girls, 80–81

Reincarnation, 59, 63
Residence patterns, 53, 54
matrilocal, 53, 82

Revitalization movements, 71–72
  Bear Lake Indians, 71, 72
  Chandalar Kutchin, 72
  Sarsi, 71
Role differentiation and decision making,
  47–49
Royal Canadian Mounted Police, 109, 114,
  115
Russian-American Co., 94, 98, 99, 102
Russian Orthodox Church, 98, 99
Sarsi (Sarcee)
  distribution of, 15
  European contact, 15
  revitalization movements, 71
Scapulimancy, 64–65
Schools, 99, 109
Sekani
  abandonment of the aged, 83
  disposal of the dead, 85
  puberty rites, boys, 80
  shamanism, 66
  warfare, 50
Service, E., 57
Settlement pattern classification, 38
  Central-Based Wanderers
    Ingalik, 41, 42
    Koyukon, 42
    Tanaina, 42
    Tanana, 42
  Restricted Wanderers
    Peel River Kutchin, 40, 41
Shamanism, 66, 67
  Chandalar Kutchin, 67, 68
  Kaska, 66
  Sekani, 66
  Tahltan, 66
  Tanaina, 67
  Upper Tanana, 69
Shamans
  duties and skills, 67–69
Sibs. See Matrilineal sib organization.
Slat armor, 51
Slave
  abandonment of the aged, 83
  death, attitudes toward, 83
  disposal of the dead, 85
  distribution of, 14
  dwellings, 35
  European contact and, 14
  leadership, 48
  naming, 78
  preferential marriage, 81
  puberty rites, girls, 80
  social groupings, 45
  subsistence, 24, 25, 26
Snowshoes, 26
Social groupings, 44, 45
  Dogrib, 45, 46, 47
  Ingalik, 45, 47
  Slave, 45
Sororate, 53
Spirits, 62, 66
Steward, J., 57
Subsistence
  Atna, 30
  Chandalar Kutchin, 26, 27
  Chipewyan, 24, 25, 26
  Eskimos, 31

Ingalik, 28, 29
Slave, 24, 25, 26
Tahltan, 27
Tanaina, 29, 30
Upper Koyukuk, 17
Vunta Kutchin, 114, 116
Yukon Flats Kutchin, 27
Sullivan, R., 129

Tagish
  influenced by Tlingit, 17
  matrilineal sib organization, 52
Tahltan
  ceremonies, 70
  disposal of the dead, 85
  fur trade, 98
  leadership, 49
  matrilineal sib organization, 52
  potlatch, 56
  puberty rites, boys, 79, 80
  shamanism, 66
  subsistence, 27
Tanaina
  beliefs about game, 21
  death, 84
  disposal of the dead, 85
  distribution of, 20
  dwellings, 36, 37
  fur trade, 29, 94, 95, 98
  matrilineal sib organization, 52
  missionary activity, 98
  preferential marriage, 81
  settlement patterns, 42
  shamanism, 67
  subsistence, 29, 30, 31
Tanana, 1, 2
  distribution of, 17, 18
  leadership, 49
  matrilineal sib organization, 52
  matrilocal residence, 53
  potlatch, 56
  settlement patterns, 42
  teknonomy, 78
  warfare, 50
Teit, J., 128
Teknonomy, 78, 79
Trade. See Fur trade.
Tsetsaut
  influenced by Tsimshian, 17
Tutchone
  fur trade, 98
  influenced by Tlingit, 17
  matrilineal sib organization, 52

Unilinear descent groups
  corporate functions of, 58
U.S. Government
  services of, 99, 109–112
Upper Koyukuk
  distribution of, 17
  subsistence, 17
Upper Tanana, 70
  beliefs about game, 21
  childbirth, 77
  death, 83, 84
  disposal of the dead, 85
  distribution of, 17
  dwellings, 33, 34, 37

fur trade, 98
leadership, 49
life cycle, 87
mythology, 61
potlatch, 55, 56
pregnancy, 76
preferential marriage, 81
puberty rites, girls, 80
shamanism, 69
warfare, 51
Urban development, 107

Vancouver, G., 94
Vunta Kutchin, 114, 116

Wage employment, 107, 109, 110, 118, 120
Warfare, 49, 50, 51
  Chandalar Kutchin, 48, 49, 50
  Chipewyan, 50
  Eskimos, 50
  Peel River Kutchin, 50
  Sekani, 50
  Tanana, 50
  Upper Tanana, 51
Welfare, 111–112, 116, 118, 119, 120
Wife sharing, 53

Yellowknife Indians, 14, 15, 92, 95
Yukon Flats Kutchin, 27